Icons of Loss and Grace

Icons
of Loss
and
Grace

Moments from the
Natural World

Susan Hanson

Illustrations by Melanie Fain

Texas Tech University Press

Copyright © 2004 by Texas Tech University Press

This book is typeset in Monotype Centaur. The acid-free paper used in this book meets the minimum requirements of ANSI/NISO Z39.48-1992 (R1997). ∞

Library of Congress Cataloging-in-Publication Data
Hanson, Susan, 1951–
  Icons of loss and grace : moments from the natural world / by Susan Hanson.
    p.   cm.
  ISBN 0-89672-522-7 (alk. paper)
  1. Natural history. I. Title.
QH81.H238 2004
508—dc22

                                          2003022131

03 04 05 06 07 08 09 10 11 / 9 8 7 6 5 4 3 2 1

Printed in the United States of America

"Icons of Loss and Grace" appeared in ISLE (Interdisciplinary Studies in Literature and Environment), Summer 2001. A small part of this essay also appeared under another title "What Is Dust" in Northern Lights, Spring 2001.
    "Why Write About Nature?" has appeared in Getting Over the Color Green (Tucson: University of Arizona Press, 2001), and in Southwestern Literature, Spring 1995.
    "A December Walk in the Woods" has appeared in different form as "Palmetto Pocket" in Texas Parks and Wildlife magazine, November 1998.

Texas Tech University Press
Box 41037
Lubbock, Texas 79409-1037 USA
800.832.4042
ttup@ttu.edu
www.ttup.ttu.edu

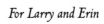

For Larry and Erin

Contents

Loss

Grace

Introduction

MY FIRST EXPERIENCE with what is now called the literature of place occurred even before I could read. The book was *Animals under Your Feet!* and it belonged to my older brother, Charles. Written by Ivah Green in 1953, it had been a gift to Charles from my mother in the summer of that same year. I was just a toddler then, but by the time I was four or five I was mesmerized by this book. Not surprisingly, what intrigued me first were the photographs—particularly the close-ups of a grimacing brown bat and a trapdoor spider at work. My interest in the words came later.

Other books would have an equal or greater impact on my life, but this is the one that initially stirred my innate curiosity about the world. Though I had no experience of bats or moles or much of anything else that Green described—save for the earthworms and ants—I was gratified to know that such things existed. Even more thrilling was the possibility that they were living right under my feet.

Over the years, I frequently smuggled the book from my brother's desk and took it off to my room to read. After one such incident, I simply forgot to take it back. Today, the book sits on my study shelf.

Partly as a result of encountering this book, and partly as a result of things beyond my control—such as being an introverted child who found solace in the natural world—I grew up with a sense of kinship with what could be called the familiar wild. Though my family occasionally traveled to see relatives in the Lower Rio Grande Valley or the southern Edwards Plateau, also known as the Texas Hill Country, the landscape in which I grew up seemed far more prosaic than these. Unlike my cousins, I had no clear spring-fed river in which to swim, no enormous trees to climb. And there were no subtropical thickets full of chachalacas and raucous green jays anywhere near my ascetic back yard. I improvised by playing on a ladder set up beside the clothesline pole, and imagining the rest.

Granted, I would eventually see the beauty of the Coastal Plain—the beauty of its marshes and estuaries, its shady pecan bottoms and live oaks hung with Spanish moss—but this recognition would take some time. Compared to more scenic Corpus Christi, where we had most recently lived, the small town I moved to in 1957 had no beach, no waterfront views, and little to endear it to a child. Roughly twenty miles inland from Matagorda Bay, it was a land of rice fields, rice driers, and pickups bearing bumper stickers admonishing all to "Eat Rice Today."

Through my first three years of school, my family and I lived in a crackerbox house on an unpaved road just south of town. It was there that I learned to ride my bike on oyster shell and to keep my eyes open for snakes and bull nettle and "asps," the stinging puss caterpillars that infested our neighbor's trees. With a few neighborhood kids to play with, and a dog patient enough to wear a canvas army surplus backpack whenever I demanded, I roamed this less than idyllic landscape as if it were a true wilderness. Sometimes I suspect that being extremely myopic helped—and I say that only partly in jest: I was learning to see things up close.

As a result, I also began to develop the awareness that what is "other," what is wild, resides not only in the exotic but in the familiar as well. It would be many years before I could articulate this sense, but in becoming intimate with the commonplace, and learning to value it, I was finding meaning in the ordinary things of this world.

Still, it is one thing to know and appreciate nature and quite another to write about it. For me, the latter began when I was in graduate school, working on a creative thesis in poetry.

Once again, the immediate landscape in which I was living was an understated one. Newly married, my husband and I could afford only the most modest of rent houses, the first on a treeless hill near a pasture full of cows and the next on a shady but neglected strip of land in town. Town, in this case, was San Marcos, a small community bisected by the Balcones Fault—Texas Hill Country rising sharply to the west and Blackland Prairie sloping eastward toward the Gulf. Located on what is now the booming Interstate 35 corridor between Austin and San Antonio, it was then a quiet college town, known primarily for its pristine river, its family-oriented theme park, and its schools.

While more dramatic natural beauties such as springs and caves lay just miles away from our home, the metaphors I chose for my poetry were domestic—new flowerbeds and muddy shoes, bats circling streetlights, the remnants of bean plants browning in the fall, the seeds of beggar's ticks, even the dead armadillo on the road. They might not be attractive in the usual sense of the word, but these were the things of my world—and any meaning I was going to find in nature would have to come through them.

Of course, this begs a very important question: Is there meaning in nature? I have long believed that there is. Perhaps this conviction comes from years of gardening and feeling the sun and soil on my skin. Perhaps it comes from those nights at church camp when I listened to the waves breaking against the shore on Tres Palacios Bay. Or maybe it's nothing more than temperament, a function of the intuitive-feeling type. I simply can't say.

What I do know, however, is that this is a way of seeing the world that feeds me.

In the culture in which I was raised, the created order existed primarily as backdrop for the human drama of sin and redemption. Lovely and useful as it might be, nature was meant to be overcome, left behind in the final triumph of the elect. Indeed, the very word *nature* implied a failure of some kind; what was natural was tainted, inferior, and, most of all, deceptive—death in the guise of life. To me, the message seemed hopelessly mixed. How could the physical world be a reflection of its Creator and a millstone around our necks? This was the sort of paradox that negated rather than nourished. I longed for something else.

Strangely enough, it was in my college freshman English class that this something else first presented itself. Accustomed as I was to a piety steeped in emotion, I warmed quickly to my instructor's off-topic discussions of Christian existentialist thought, that of theologian Paul Tillich in particular. I appreciated the fact that in Tillich's mind, questions and doubts were not just tolerated but were actually welcomed and expected. More than that, I savored the discovery that one's sense of meaning in life is not so much found as made; the notion of meaning as an absolute, something akin to ore that must be resolutely pried from rock, gradually began to recede. In its place came a growing awareness that what Tillich called the Ground of Being was not disguised or buried. Indeed, this Ground was not only right there under our feet but also in front of our eyes.

Unlike the contradictions I had experienced previously, this was a paradox I could live with—that which cannot be spoken, communicated by all that exists; that which cannot be known, made as real to us as our breath. Disquieting though it was to think on such things, I found a good companion in the works of Trappist monk and poet Thomas Merton. Particularly through *New Seeds of Contemplation*, I began to see these apparent inconsistencies as sources of nurture and hope, rich with possibility, inexhaustible. To Merton, I discovered, faith was neither a feeling nor an opinion but rather an experience of immersion, the heart and mind integrated and living within the divine. Meaning came not from rejecting the world but from participating in its ongoing creation. Mystery was encountered not in some ethereal realm but in the tangible things of this earth. As Merton put it, "Everything that is, is holy."

To say that matter itself is sacred, and therefore capable of communicating the numinous, is, of course, to invite all manner of labels: Platonic, pantheistic, pagan. I am none of the above. Rather, I count myself as part of an ancient sacramental tradition that embraces the physical and the spiritual, that sees them as an undivided whole and therefore equally real. In "The Wilderness," British poet Kathleen Raine announces:

> *I have glimpsed the bright mountain behind the mountain,*
> *Knowledge under the leaves, tasted the bitter berries red,*
> *Drunk cold water and clear from an inexhaustible hidden fountain.*

The key words here, I believe, are *glimpsed* and *tasted*. Raine can make no claim to having seen the full picture or having satiated her thirst. All vision is partial, she acknowledges, and the image invariably arrives in pieces. There is a "mountain behind the mountain," Raine would argue, but apprehending it requires that one first experience what Noel Dermot O'Donoghue has described as the "ordinary, very physical, very material mountain."

In the Eastern Orthodox tradition, nothing captures this principle more aptly than the icon. An artistic and spiritual representation of a holy person or event, the icon does more than portray an image. It communicates a reality—the mountain behind the mountain, if you will. Often described as "a meeting between heaven and earth," the icon invites the participation of the beholder; while maintaining its own integrity as a thing in itself, the icon functions as a window into what poet Gerard Manley Hopkins referred to as "the dearest freshness deep down things."

To see the natural world as an icon, then, is to see meaning in the most ordinary of things. Embedded in all that is, the numinous communicates itself through encounters with the familiar wild—with titmice at a window feeder, with the butterfly caught in a spider's web, with gaillardia in full bloom. To experience such encounters is not to have visions or to hear voices but, rather, to catch a glimpse of that which animates all. For me, at least, these moments of awareness always come and go in a flash. There is nothing spectacular about them, and yet it is in them that I see how pain can evolve into grace.

Keeping a record of such encounters is a habit I developed many years ago. While working for the San Marcos *Daily Record*, I wrote not only feature articles and reviews but also a column called "Notes in Passing." Every Friday for roughly fifteen years, I shared my opinions, laughed at my latest failures in the classroom or at home, and tried to make sense of the losses in my life. In doing the latter, I frequently found myself returning to the images and metaphors I knew best—my garden, the local flora and fauna, the Texas landscape in general. This natural inclination on my part, coupled with the editor's injunctions to "write short," yielded a kind of hybrid—personal essays that relied heavily on the conventions of poetry.

What follows is a collection of those essays, many of which first appeared in very different form. Written as reflections, rather than full-blown arguments or exhaustive accounts of how one resolves the questions of love and loss, they are partial responses at best. Indeed, resolution itself is imperfect, taking us only as far as the next moment of disclosure, and the next. As Rainer Maria Rilke puts it in his *Book of Hours*, "I live my life in widening circles / that reach out across the world." We cover our ground not once, but again and again. The same birds, the same trees, the same slant of sun on a summer afternoon—they are all the signs we have.

If we choose to read them—and the choice is very much ours—we must remember to do so slowly. We must be patient, reminding ourselves that whatever comes will arrive a piece at a time. And finally, we must bear the weight of paradox, recognizing that delight and sorrow are soul mates, that redemption and loss are a part of the same sacred ground.

Innocence

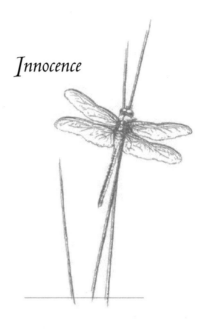

Instructed by a Seed
Or, How the Garden Tells Us
What It Knows

FIRST THERE IS only the cool, bare soil, and then a slender filament of green. Bursting through the surface, it stretches sunward, gradually unfolding as a wispy whorl of leaves.

Another *Cosmos bipinnatus* has been born.

"I often wonder what it feels like to the seed," my gardening friend says, musing on the process. "Rather like giving birth, I suspect."

Closing my eyes, I imagine the event in slow motion—and with sound. It begins with the explosion of the seed wall, with the crashing of an embryonic leaf into the dark and fertile soil. Quickened by the sun, the epicotyl presses up toward light and air. Drawn by what it neither sees nor understands, it rises blindly to the surface of the earth.

Heaving, creaking, the substance of the world is rent asunder by a seed. And in the end, a single blade of green is left as testimony to the process we call Life.

What does it feel like to the seed? Like birth, perhaps, or more like death? Like something that it's never done before, yet knows? Like what the seed was made to be?

These were hardly the sorts of questions I considered as a novice gardener. Only six when I began to turn and till the soil, I was more concerned with the tenacity of Johnson grass roots and the gumminess of heavy Gulf Coast clay.

Kneeling in my little garden at the east end of our small frame house, I had no knowledge of such things as friability or tilth, microbial activity or humus. I had no words for the way the soil would cake up on the soles of my once-white Keds or work itself below the cuticles of my nails. I had no understanding of the sort of chemistry that caused the soil to come together in a clod, to gather weight and density, to coalesce like stone.

If I added water to a certain type of clay, I learned, the result was a primitive sort of burnt orange paint. It was this that I used to coat the flimsy wooden fence around my garden, this that turned the heels of my hands a funny shade of brown.

What I knew about gardening at that age, in short, was purely experiential. Barely able to read and write, too literal minded for abstract thought, I reveled in the sensuality of childhood. The world was a potpourri of textures and smells, of colors and tastes and sounds. It was the scent of fresh-cut grass and dirt and oyster shell crackling beneath the tires of my old blue bike. It was everything that pressed against my skin, everything immediate, everything, as Hopkins wrote, "original, spare, strange."

Perhaps it was a function of being nearsighted, but I found myself particularly entranced by little things. Being myopic, I discovered, was a gift. Get down close enough, I learned, and the world became a universe; each twig, each leaf, each inch of soil became a cosmos.

What intrigued me more than anything, though, was the germination of the seeds I planted every spring. As a rule, they were simply pinto beans taken from my mother's stockpile on the kitchen shelf, but that was part of the mystery. How could something so hard, so unyielding, so plain metamorphose into something supple, beautiful, alive?

I couldn't understand, but child that I was, I could enjoy.

These days, I confess, I am far less literal than that. These days when I garden, I am far more prone to speculate about the earth as metaphor, to find not only pleasure in the seasons but meaning, too.

"All our gardens are expressions of what we were, tempered by what we are, what we have and what we want," Jennifer Bennett writes in *Our Gardens Ourselves*. Or, as Henry Beston put it, "A garden is a mirror of the mind."

What, I must ask, does my garden say of me? The winding paths, the piles of stone, the toad that sleeps beneath the weathered railroad tie—what sort of mind do they reflect? These are the questions I consider as I set aside my grubbing hoe and rake, as I press the soil around the supple roots of lemon grass, as I live my one and only life.

For more than twenty years now, my husband and I have made our home on a wooded acre six miles south of town. Rangeland turned to residential lots, our subdivision skirts an ancient fault line separating Texas Blackland Prairie to the east and Edwards Plateau limestone to the west. The shelf of rock that runs beneath our front yard's meager crust of soil has left no question as to where our own land lies.

Raised as I was in a country far more lush than this, in a geography of rice fields and pecan bottoms and oak trees draped with Spanish moss, I had no firsthand knowledge of what this rocky land would bear. It didn't take long to learn.

In my first few months here, I would watch as, one by one, the plants I'd loved since childhood turned chlorotic, wilted, and died. Starved by the chalky, alkaline soil, the azaleas and gardenias never thrived the way they had back in the gardens of my youth. Doomed before I even put them in the ground, the hydrangeas withered, turning brittle in the searing August sun.

This land was harder than I knew.

Or was it?

"We left this Mexican buckeye here for you," I recalled the realtor saying as he led us on a walking tour of our lot. I had had no inkling what a buckeye was back then, but the knowledge that the builder had seen fit to leave it where it was pleased me nonetheless. Something beautiful, I reasoned, was at home in this terrain; something beautiful, I concluded, could survive.

But it was only when the last gardenia died, when the Chinese tallow froze and the lawn succumbed to cold and drought—it was only then that I let the buckeye start to teach me what it knew.

"Commonly found in rocky areas in canyons and on slopes in south-central and southwest Texas, east to Dallas County and west to the Trans-Pecos," horticulturalist Jill Nokes writes of the small native tree. "Mexican buckeye prefers well-drained soil and will grow in either full sun or partial shade. It is drought tolerant and will thrive in areas with limited rainfall."

Though not a true buckeye, this member of the soapberry family bears seeds resembling those of its namesake tree. "Fruits are woody pods containing as many as three round, shiny black seeds," writes Nokes, who adds that they will germinate quite easily in only a few short weeks.

So what can such a tree teach? Indeed, what can it know at all? The questions are baffling at best.

Having discovered that the Mexican buckeye flourished where exotic plants would not, I set out to do a species inventory of our lot. The list began with the obvious plants—the live oaks and the hackberry trees, the cedar elms and Ashe juniper, the dewberries and red yucca, the mountain laurel, agarita, prickly pear, and mustang grapes.

Less familiar, but no less easy to spot, were the Mexican persimmon and the sumacs—prairie flameleaf, aromatic, and evergreen. Other species would require more time to classify, more hours with the field guides I was reading well into the night.

These plants, I would learn, had names like tickle tongue or toothache tree, elbowbush, skunk bush or common hop tree, Texas snakewood or hog plum, thorn-crested agave, soapberry, and la coma. These were their common names, of course, names full of ancient and practical wisdom, names rich with the stories of place.

And what did these stories reveal? The message was simple at first: Force never carries the day. Determined as I had been to recreate my Gulf Coast landscape here on rocky ground, the soil had other plans.

The gardenias and azaleas might humor me for a while, but a life more suited to this place would win out in the end.

I learned the lesson soon enough. What has taken longer, I confess, is my grasping of the subtext written in this land.

In *Second Nature: A Gardener's Education*, Michael Pollan writes of his own transformation from guilt-ridden lawn slave to emancipated gardener. His father's rebellion notwithstanding, Pollan had been nurtured on the notion of control; the clipped and tidy landscape, with its "foundation plantings" and its unbroken swath of grass, was part of the American dream. To reject it, he learned, was to break a social covenant, to violate a code.

In time, however, Pollan grew to understand a very different way of tending to the earth. "Gardening, I had by now come to appreciate, is a painstaking exploration of place," he writes. "Gardening, as compared to lawn care, tutors us in nature's ways, fostering an ethic of give-and-take with respect to the land. Gardens instruct us in the particularities of place."

Having failed to turn his garden into something it was not, Pollan began to learn the virtues of watchful waiting, of patience, of relinquishing control. And so, at last, had I.

Tired of doing battle with this land, I looked for patterns in the way its flora grew and changed. Instead of treating every unknown seedling as a weed, I let it be—at least until I knew for certain what it was. And rather than imposing some design more suited to a different time and place, I let the landscape show me how it worked.

I won't pretend that I am always pleased with the results. I will readily admit, for instance, to cutting out the greenbriar when it grows too near the house, or trimming back the elbowbush when it arcs too near the drive. I will confess to yanking out the ubiquitous seedlings of hackberry trees and cedar elms. And I will candidly declare that I find pleasure in the pulling up of beggar's ticks and grassburs, henbit and stickygrass.

The urge to put my own stamp on this place is hard to quell.

And yet, I also know this simple premise to be true: Just as surely as I am making a garden in this place, that garden is making me.

There is in children, theologian Sallie McFague observes, an unself-conscious naiveté about the natural world, "a wide-eyed curiosity about it, as well as identification with it." For the child, she writes, the boundary between the self and the other is permeable, if not absent altogether.

"It is not a state to which we can return, much as romantics and deep ecologists wish we might," McFague argues. "Rather, our task is to attempt the second naiveté, a return to connection with others that recognizes distance and respects differences."

In describing what she calls this "second naiveté," McFague writes: "It is as if the world-openness of childhood, that sense of interest in and closeness with all others, had now gone to school; it is to be educated to understand how difficult it is to really know others in their otherness and also to feel genuine bonds of affection for them—as they are."

Transplanting Turk's cap from one bed to another, sowing seeds of horsemint or gaillardia or Gulf Coast penstemon, I am conscious of the kinship binding me to them. We are, in the most fundamental sense, a community of lives. They are not part of me, nor I of them; it's hardly as simple as that. We are, though, social beings, emerging, changing, taking shape in terms of what is growing next to us. My garden tells me this.

At the edge of the woods where the tickle tongue used to be, a cedar elm grows out around the oaks, ungainly in its search for sun and air. Missouri violets, preferring the soapberry's shade, seed out among the leaves of last year's *Salvia coccinea*. Beneath the mountain cedar, or Ashe juniper, nothing chooses to grow at all.

This is not the garden that I dreamed of in my youth, but it is the garden that has grown out of my life.

Pulling seed heads off the greenthread still blooming in the ditch, I will fling them out across the late spring grass. I will sprinkle them among the winecups and gaillardia, among the beebalm and the Drummond's phlox. Then I will hope for rain and wait.

Like the words of a prayer that is spoken in the dark, these seeds I sow will change me as they germinate and grow. These seeds will answer with a mystery I can live into but never fully know.

To garden, I have realized, is to make a space for what we cannot understand. In moving toward Sallie McFague's second naiveté, I am, in essence, moving toward my self. It is the work of middle age.

How appropriate, I think as I transplant coralberry to a shady spot beneath the oaks. How appropriate, how true. No longer the novice gardener, the child who melded with the earth, no longer the apprentice bent on turning native landscapes into something they are not, I am more content these days to listen and to wait. These days I am pleased to let the caterpillars take their share of buckeye leaves and dill, to let the winter honeysuckle crawl across the lawn, to let zexmenia and yarrow and penstemon come up where they will. These days, in hopes of being faithful to my one and only life, I let my garden speak.

The Act of Attention

S HE IS DOING tai chi in the middle of the path.

What is the proper etiquette for this? I wonder. Do I stand here, pretending to admire the bark of the nearest tree? Do I ignore her and simply walk right by, training my eyes on the ground ahead?

I am stumped, I'll admit—and more annoyed than I care to say.

Young and thin, the woman appears to be very much at home with herself. Like me, she has been at this South Texas retreat center for several days now. But unlike me, she wears a certain lightness, a grace that bespeaks a kind of inner calm.

I am wearing a backpack full of books.

Pausing on the sandy path that winds some two miles through the trees, I watch her for a moment, watch her standing with her arms raised in the air like wings. She has become a crane.

Not knowing how long she will pose there, readying herself for flight, I decide I have no choice but to slip discreetly by. Holding my camera close against my chest, and keeping my eyes on the path, I follow the wheel rut to the right. I am careful not to make a sound, not to let my clothing rustle, not to breathe more loudly than I should.

The woman simply stands there, motionless and mute.

What annoys me, I realize as I walk, is that this woman's practice isn't mine. Lissome as the saplings growing underneath the oaks, she has a grace I envy, a composure I imagine that I lack. Somehow, I suspect, her way of working toward the center of her life is far more enlightening than mine.

Rounding the corner, and passing a deer trail through the brush, I watch for the sign that will mark a pathway to my left. For several mornings now, I have taken this detour to a pond beyond a motte of oaks and palms. And for several mornings, I have waded through the young spring grass, set up my campstool just behind a screen of reeds, and waited for the birds.

On my first day here, I encountered several blue-winged teal, the male distinguished by the stripe of white between his bill and eyes. Gliding back and forth across the pond, the birds seemed oblivious not only to the turtle sunning on the muddy bank but also to the Wied's crested flycatcher, snatching insects as it tumbled through the air.

This morning, though, there are no ducks. I find a colony of cormorants instead.

"Five cormorants are swimming in the pond today," I note in the journal I hold balanced on my lap, "five cormorants like a haiku skimming the surface, grinning apostrophes on water."

While I am not looking, they all get out, flex their wings, and then run back into the water like children, splashing one another as they go. If it weren't anthropocentric to do so, I'd say these creatures were in love with the lives they lead.

Taking a closer look, I see that my count is wrong. "There are ten, not five," I write at the bottom of the page. "Cormorants on holiday, I guess."

A comical lot, these birds wear perpetual grins. With their upturned bills and their snakelike necks, they ride low in the water like loons. It seems fitting, then, to read in my 1951 *Audubon Water Bird Guide* that when double-crested cormorants are first hatched, "the naked, coal-black young look like rubber toys." They are not much different now.

Perched on my stool, and out of their line of sight, I make a small confession in my book. "I feel a bit like a voyeur," I write as a final note, "sneaking up on a group of bathers skinny-dipping in the pond."

Leaving the birds to their play, I fold up my stool, place my journal in my pack, and head back down the trail the way I came. Best not to be too quiet, I think, padding silently on the sand. In the grass, at the edge of the path, a javelina stares at me, turns, and trots into the brush on stiff-legged tiptoe.

Within minutes, I am veering past a pile of deer dung on the trail. Instead of walking on, though, I stop to watch a pair of beetles struggling to carry a single pellet away. Ignoring the shadow of my boots, they roll it toward a clump of straggler daisies near the path. And there, while I stoop to see exactly how they work, they bury the dung in the sand.

What is my practice? I wonder as I think back to the young woman on the path. *What is authentic life for me?* All too often I've imagined that the answer lay in reading the right book, finding the right program, emulating the right spiritual guide. But I've found it in none of these.

In a key episode in his novel *The Dharma Bums*, Jack Kerouac follows Ryder Japhy, Henry Morley, and narrator Ray Smith as they attempt to ascend a mountain in the Sierra Nevada. After a day of climbing has taken them to the foot of Matterhorn peak, the trio must decide whether to continue toward the summit or begin the descent toward camp. Smith and Japhy elect to go on.

Novice climber that he is, Smith has been duly impressed by the grace and agility with which Japhy leaps from rock to rock. Earlier, in fact, he had tried to copy his friend's technique, finally realizing that he would be more successful if he were simply to "pick [his] own boulders and make a ragged dance of [his] own."

It is only on the way down, however, that Smith actually gets it. Having clambered almost to the top of the Matterhorn, he makes his descent with joyful abandon, intuitively creating his route through the rocks as he goes. All of a sudden, Smith exclaims, "everything was just like jazz." No longer worried about how his performance compares to Japhy's, he is at last free to experience his life as his own. Like the jazz musician, Smith is finally letting the music come, naturally flowing from a center that is deep within himself.

What might my life be like were I to give in to the rhythms of my own ragged dance? Like this, I imagine, walking down the trail, past grapevines and winecups and huisache blooming in the sun. Just like this attentiveness, this pleasure, this being present to the world.

Where It All Begins

THE CATS' WATER BOWL is full of birds. First a cardinal, blazing red even in the dim light of the morning, then a troop of sparrows. One after another they hop in, disappear in a blur of water, then spring up to the nearest branch to sun themselves and tweak every feather into place.

This is where it begins. In a bowl of water. On a morning full of birds. With the sun barely over the treetops, barely over the galvanized roof of the shed. With leaves fallen and blown into a single row.

This is where it always begins. With a leaf floating in a bowl of water. Presided over by birds. With the sun on a galvanized roof. Feathers, red, and every one in place.

It is the daily rearrangement of the world. Like poetry, the pieces gather into lines—curved lines, curved the way that cat ears arch toward sound, the way that shadows wrap themselves around the leaves of trees.

All the parts, even the frayed ones, are used.

It is morning when I walk to the back of the garden, morning when I spot the clump of baby blue eyes sprawled across the rich black earth. Unexpected there between the Clary sage and the garlic chives, the rosemary and the southernwood, it is blooming with the hyacinth and the winter honeysuckle, blooming with the first of spring still weeks away.

This place is the place where I live.

This year, I imagine, I will grow sestinas in the patch of soil below the neighbor's chain-link fence. I will watch them push up through the earth, watch them as they climb, sweet and supple, wrapping hold-fasts on the wire mesh between the pointed posts. By June, if the sun and rain are right, they'll be twining in the top of the long-dead sumac, straining toward the light.

Closer in, just beyond the birdbath, couplets will emerge full grown. Buried like bulbs since fall, they'll have spent the winter growing underground, forming themselves into words. Come spring, they'll rise up tall as sentences, as lines—straight this time—straight as the stems of daffodils, and just as green.

Already, sonnets are sprouting from the compost. Last year's orange peels, potato skins, and grapefruit rinds; seeds from a water-melon served on a summer night; peach pits and bad tomatoes, bought and forgotten at the back of the refrigerator; a crust of bread; chickweed pulled from a backyard flowerbed; old spaghetti; coffee grounds from Sunday a week ago, when it was colder and the house felt damp and chill; four eggshells, crushed; a piece of twine; leftover salad, gone limp and brown; leaves raked from the front yard one Sat-urday at noon; broccoli stems; the remnants of a squash—reduced to fundamentals, reduced by sun and rain and creatures visiting at night, these leavings of the world are all the things I love.

Turned and lifted, turned and left to settle on themselves, they are slowly changing into verse. Pressed, pungent as shards of garlic, they too are words, ripe for picking from the earth.

This is where it begins, this urge to know the world, to put its see-smell-taste-touch-hear into something we can say. Like "Good morning," or "It looks like rain today," or, if we forget the rules of logic for a moment, "The sun sounds like the songs of birds."

Driven out of our kitchens, or away from our computers, driven from the television or the sofa or the bed, we rip off our shoes and run our unshod feet, soft as cats' paws, through the grass. Creatures too, we sense there's something going on beyond the double panes of glass, beyond the deck, beyond ourselves. There is something going on, we imagine, something kin to the way our blood runs, to the way the air fills our lungs and comes out again, to the way our skin tingles when surprised.

It is life, we imagine, visceral and sweet and clear. Urged to poetry, we bury our hands in the earth and pull out words. Singing, we gather the wealth of the world.

The Migration of Cranes

I AM SITTING in the backyard swing, watching a frenzied knot of sparrows at the feeder, when I hear a strange but familiar sound. *Jays*, I think at first, imagining them somewhere far away, calling, perhaps, from behind a row of trees or houses, from behind the air itself.

And then I hear it again. Too high, too thin, too delicate to be jays, this sound is coming from another world.

Cranes. The recognition hits me just the way that fire registers itself upon a hand. *Sandhill cranes.*

If smell is the most primitive of senses, triggering a lifetime's worth of memories with a single scent—bacon frying in a pan, wet sycamores, a Christmas candle burning on a table in the hall—then hearing follows close behind. Play a line from a familiar song, and the mind cannot remember where it is. It might be a day when you were six, and it was raining, and your mother was fixing dinner in the other room. Or, just as easily, it might be a Saturday in May, when you were driving in your car, not noticing where you were, not thinking anything at all.

Sounds play tricks on us like this.

Hearing the sandhill cranes, I run inside, find my binoculars, and head to the front of the house. There, standing at the end of the drive, I turn my face toward the south, toward the sky, toward a dome of incredible blue.

The light is more than I can bear.

Temporarily blinded by the sun, I close my eyes and listen hard, listen for the bugling of the cranes.

"There is no more thrilling sound in wild America," writes John Tveten in *The Birds of Texas*. "Over the sound of the prairie wind comes the rolling, trumpeting cry, *gar-oo-oo gar-oo-oo*, echoing back and forth within the flock."

Having located the birds by ear, I am able, at last, to pinpoint their place in the sky. There, almost directly overhead, is a ragged V of seven birds. *Just seven?* I lift my glasses and count the cranes again. The sound of the flock is far greater than its size.

"If the whooping cranes are the aristocrats of Texas birds," Tveten notes, "then the sandhills are Everyman's birds." And that they truly are.

Though whoopers number only about three hundred, the population of sandhill cranes is relatively large. Each year, ornithologists estimate, well over half a million of them make their way from breeding grounds in Canada and Alaska down to the southwestern United States. While many overwinter at the Bitter Lake Wildlife Refuge in New Mexico, or at the Muleshoe National Wildlife Refuge farther east, thousands more head south to the Texas coast or the lower Rio Grande.

There, as Tveten puts it, they "stalk majestically through open marshes and grasslands, feeding on a cosmopolitan diet of small animals and aquatic life, insects, grain, green shoots and berries." There, they wait for their cue to fly north.

Two years ago, in a stretch of South Texas scrub, I happened across a trio of sandhill cranes wading silently through a slough. Ignoring the pintails and the coots, the single American wigeon and the pair of buffleheads bobbing up and down on the pond, the cranes spent a good half hour feeding at the edges in the grass.

Unlike whooping cranes, which are white and more than four feet tall, the members of this threesome were gray and sported a red patch just above the eyes. Even at a distance, there was no mistaking what they were. Still, I was caught off guard when, in a matter of seconds, they became alarmed, flapped their wings, and rose from the pond in flight. "When they took off and gar-oo-oo'd their call," I wrote in my journal later on, "I realized that they and not geese were what I heard on my walk yesterday."

Writing of this creature in *A Sand County Almanac*, Aldo Leopold saw in the comings and goings of the sandhill crane the "ticking of the geologic clock." When we hear this call, he wrote, "we hear no mere bird. He is a symbol of our untamable past, of that incredible sweep of millennia which underlies and conditions the daily affairs of birds and men."

Indeed, when we hear the call of the sandhill crane, heading north along the Central Flyway on a breezy day in March, or bound for southern marshes in the fall, we are hearing a creature of the Eocene, a remnant of the earth's most ancient life.

Standing on my driveway on a crisp October day, straining to see a line of seven sandhill cranes, I find it easy to imagine how people once believed that souls were carried heavenward by cranes. Hearing their call, I imagine a memory of my own most primal self.

Gar-oo-oo gar-oo-oo, they sing, the notes rolling thin and sweet from somewhere overhead. And as they sing, I feel my soul rise, weightless, restless, yearning for the sky.

Dayflowers

PARTIAL TO MOISTURE AND SHADE, false dayflower rises from the winter beds luxuriant and lush. Then, for the first month or so of its life, it does nothing dramatic at all—nothing, that is, save for swathing the yard in green.

In short, I'm always glad to see it sprout, always ready for the change its presence signals in the earth. But welcome as it is in early spring, before the redbuds bloom and the cedar elms leaf out, *Commelinantia anomala* looks bedraggled in this second week of May.

Clearly, it is past its prime.

"Did you plant that?" my husband's cousin asked while visiting here two weeks ago. I had to laugh.

"It's a weed," I told him, trying to remember that his home in Colorado had gotten snow just days before. Anything in bloom this time of year, I suspected, would look beautiful to him.

"It grows pretty much like grass," I continued. "Takes over if you let it." And indeed, take over is what it had done.

Roughly two feet tall, false dayflower was growing from one corner of the yard to the other—under the soapberries and the pear, under the peach tree and the plum, in and out of the mountain laurels, among the vinca and the iris and the oak. While my guest stood back and watched, I began pulling it out in clumps.

Two weeks later, I'm at the job still.

Unlike true dayflower, or widow's tears, false dayflower is an annual, its flower distinctly more lavender than blue. An even more telling clue to its identity, however, is the arrangement of its two larger petals and three upper stamens, which look for all the world like a nose and two fuzzy yellow eyes.

Yanking it out by the handfuls, I glance away from the tiny face. This isn't personal, after all.

Welcome in one season, rejected in the next—the false dayflower that had brightened my early spring has suddenly become a bane. But isn't that the way weeds are? Plants unappreciated, uninvited, wrong for this or that specific space?

This plant, it occurs to me, is really no more a weed than any of the natives growing in the flowerbed out front. Gaillardia and pink evening primrose, Texas thistle and greenthread, winecup and horsemint, Gulf Coast penstemon and mealy blue sage, Texas star and skullcap, Engelmann's daisy and gaura, ox-eye daisy and zexmenia, the last of the bluebonnets and the yarrow—might they be weeds as well?

Visiting native plant nurseries these days, I seldom fail to go away amused—and more than a little smug. "We have a yard full of this," I mutter to my husband as we pass a row of spiderwort or greenthread. Why, even the straggler daisies, which I pull by the fistfuls from underneath my roses, are suddenly for sale.

So when is a weed a weed?

"I could help you with this," my brother-in-law offered on a visit several years ago. Standing on our backyard deck, surveying what struck him as a jungle, he frowned at the chest-high stands of sunflower goldeneye, the clumps of agarita, persimmon, and sage. "A good lawnmower is all you'd need."

His tone was light, but his message was sincere. Where I had seen native, natural, low-maintenance, he had seen something very different. He had seen a patch of weeds.

Curious about what was native to this place, I decided years ago to give the mystery plants a chance. As a result, we now have a trio of soapberry trees, each roughly twenty feet in height. And we have a host of other things as well—the littleleaf mulberry in the woods, the elbowbush in front of my study window and in the bed out back, the clump of toothache trees beside the peach.

Not all of the surprises, though, were quite so worthy of note.

The year I convinced myself that we had a remarkable stand of castor beans, for instance, we in fact had a grove of giant ragweed. And another year, all the infant "gaillardias" I pampered by the fence turned out to be a still nameless plant bearing stickers instead of blooms. These days, I snatch it out the second it appears.

Other strays—other surprises—I can take or leave at will. What harm, for example, has three-seeded mercury ever done? Or trompillo? Granted, the latter produces supposedly poisonous fruit, and stems that are stickery to the touch, but I'm happy to leave it alone. The scarlet spiderling running through the ditch, the pepper-vine and catbriar and Carolina snailseed—each can be a pest, all right, but I have to ask for whom?

Not for the titmice flitting through the tangle of vines, or the butterflies, or the ladybug crawling up the stem. And not for the host of other creatures for whom these outcasts constitute the world.

And so, you might say, I've reached a compromise with weeds. Yes, I pull the false dayflower—eventually, and only when it's started to grow limp and to fade and, finally, to go to seed. And I keep a path cut for myself and my husband and the pets to walk through the shaggy yard.

But otherwise, hospitality's the rule at my house. Just as there's room for the possum that lives under our shed and the squirrels that squander our bird seed, there's space for a common weed or two, for the dandelions and thistles, the goldenrod and old man's beard. There's room, in short, for what is unkempt, lowly, and wild. Even the uninvited, I have learned, have remarkable gifts to bring.

Angles and Edges

Iᴛ's ᴛʜᴇ ᴀɴɢʟᴇs ᴏғ ᴛʜɪɴɢs that I notice, the lip of a roof line curving in the blue of an April sky, the edge of a shadow inching out from underneath a bench.

Walking down the hall past the classroom where I teach, I catch myself glancing out of a window, glancing toward the turret of a building that I've seen a thousand times before. For some reason I can't name, it catches my eye today. For some reason, I am caught by the crispness of the image, by the slick rim of a blue sky pressed against a red tile roof.

Angles. Edges. The way things come together. It is the architecture of the morning that intrigues me so, the placement of arcs and lines and subtle shafts of light.

"Did you take all these?" a student asks, staring at the photos on my office wall.

Yes, I tell her, wondering if she'll notice what I finally saw in them not long ago. Five unrelated photographs: except for the fact that each is in black and white, they seem to have nothing in common. Or so I used to think.

One of them, taken four or five years ago, shows an open gate off a highway in northern New Mexico, an open gate and a rutted road leading through a grassy pasture toward the hills. Another, shot in Turret, Colorado, invites the eye through the door of an abandoned house, then through an interior door, then through a window out into the woods. In yet another, South Texas sun and shade define a row of arches holding up the roof of a cool veranda. The fourth, a photo of my daughter, shows her silhouetted, lying under a wisp of cloud on an L-shaped slab of granite, knees bent, hands shielding her eyes from the desert sun. In the last, a single bristlecone pine arches eastward, while below it, all of Colorado's South Park rolls out, empty and endless, fading into haze.

These photos have hung on my office wall for years now, and for years I have failed to see just what it is they share. Not long ago, however, I realized at last that each is an invitation, a call to venture out— or in. Gates and arches, windows and doors, the line dividing rock and sky—edge places that they are, they urge me to move along, to let myself be drawn, or dragged, across some threshold in my life.

When I was a child, growing up just twenty minutes from the Texas coast, I spent a good many weekends at the beach. Despite that fact, however, I never learned to like the open Gulf. Except for those occasions when my sister dragged me laughing and screaming through the surf, I seldom ventured far from shore.

It was the tidal flats I loved, the place where the waves swept in and out, leaving behind the husks of snails and clams. Wriggling my toes into the mucky sand, I pried out the tiny shells, collected them in squatty coffee cans, and took them home to rinse off on the lawn.

What I didn't know then, but could only sense, is that those flats were places where life abounds. "The shore is an ancient world," Rachel Carson writes in *The Edge of the Sea;* "for as long as there has been an earth and sea there has been this place of the meeting of land and water. Yet it is a world that keeps alive the sense of continuing creation and of the relentless drive of life."

Constantly changing, constantly renewing itself, this edge of the sea is a marginal world indeed. It has, as Carson calls it, a dual nature, not either-or but both. Sometimes land, sometimes sea, it is a place where creatures from two different worlds connect.

Living where I do now, hours from any beach, I dwell on the margins still.

"You can barely see the house," a young friend said the other night as we stood talking in my driveway. It was an exaggeration, I realized, but not by much. My house is being swallowed by the trees. Glancing through my study window, I try to remember what it looked like years before. I try to envision the sunny green lawn, and the empty space where a forty-foot oak now stands. I can't.

What I see, instead, are edges.

Haphazardly planned, the garden that has evolved these last two decades is a hodgepodge of flowerbeds, fences, and paths. Instructed by the pets, which already had worn a track around the house, my husband and I began our landscaping by constructing a gravel walkway in its place. Other edges would follow in time—the split-rail fence, dividing the yard from the ditch; the circular bench at the base of the Spanish oak; the arch for the climbing red rose.

I can only guess what lives in the woods by our house, but I know what dwells on the edge. One such creature, a rufous-sided towhee, spent the winter churning through the leaves beside the path. Another, a brown thrasher, still appears almost daily at a feeder not far from the brush.

Who is watching whom? I sometimes wonder, as a squirrel stares at me through my study window, or a possum sights us through the back door glass. Who is the Other, when you're living on the edge?

Attempting to explain the American love affair with lawns, some sociobiologists have suggested that human beings are inherently drawn to open spaces where they can see the dangers around them. Proponents of the "savanna syndrome," as it's called, maintain that this affinity for large expanses of grass had its roots in Africa, where human survival depended on the ability to spot a predator while it was still some distance away.

Though the theory makes sense, there are times when it simply doesn't work. Years ago, for example, I discovered a small boy wandering aimlessly through my back yard. "Hi," I said, trying not to scare him. "What are you doing?" His matter-of-fact reply: "I'm walking through the woods."

What had drawn this boy to my yard wasn't a neatly trimmed blanket of St. Augustine grass but, rather, a series of messy edges. Winding through the oaks, behind the elbowbush, and past the mountain laurel, the garden path had invited the child to come in, to experience life at the border of woodland and lawn. It had promised him surprise, for that's what margins do.

Sometimes, when I look at the world just right, I can pick out the edges of things. Soil and sky meet as a ragged horizon. Water converges with stone. Spirit spills into flesh and bone, and all of it glows like glass, like a freshly polished window glinting in the sun.

In the Celtic tradition, such margins are known as "thin places," sites where the eternal and the transitory merge. Rich and textured and real, they are the spaces in between, the silence that follows a question, the light that appears just at dawn.

Standing at the open door, scanning the back yard for birds, I imagine a world of thresholds, of trees and rocks and feathers all inviting me to come up close. I imagine myself, a child again, feeling the cool earth under my feet, the scent of honeysuckle lingering on my hands. Enticed by the prospect of surprise, I step through the door into morning, toward the angles and edges of day.

Small World

L OOKS LIKE THE FOOD CHAIN at work," my husband said as
we stood above the gruesome sight. Having caught the scent
of something dead, we had wandered through the yard for a
good ten minutes before finding the remnants of a possum right on
the path by the deck. Already, maggots were stripping the carcass
clean.

Obviously dragged up by something, the creature was at this point
little more than a wad of tangled fur and a mat of broken bones. Only
the hairless tail and narrow jaw told us what it was. Or, rather, what it
had been.

Going back inside the house, I returned a moment later with the
magnifying glass I keep handy on the hutch. Bending closer to the
path, my husband and I were intrigued by what we saw. Fire ants,
working solo and in teams, were busy dragging individual maggots to
their nest beneath a stepping stone. Half the size of the larvae, the
ants were often outpowered and, for a moment at least, inadvertently
dragged away themselves.

In each case, though, the teamwork of the ants prevailed. It sometimes took two or even three of the fire ants to get the job done, but
they managed, at last, to overcome their prey and wedge the maggots
down the tunnel toward their nest.

Apparently oblivious to the drama around them, a dozen or so pillbugs congregated on the edges of the feast, somehow avoiding both
the maggots and the ants. Content to work at their usual lumbering

pace, these armor-plated isopods were in fact in little danger from the ants, and thus of little interest or concern. What those tiny predators couldn't eat, it seemed, they chose to leave alone.

Days later now, as I think back on this scene, I'm as impressed as ever by the ants, by their industry and strength. But it's the pillbugs, I'll admit, that intrigue me the most.

Crustaceans, and therefore more closely kin to crabs and shrimp than to either the maggots or the ants on that backyard path, pillbugs are an odd, intriguing lot. Referred to by children everywhere as roly-polies or doodlebugs, *Armadillidium vulgare* are perhaps best known for their entertaining habit of turning themselves into tight little balls when threatened. This defensive mechanism may work well against spiders and other would-be foes, but it only makes the creature that much more appealing to children, who troll the yard with mayonnaise jars full of grass.

Next to fireflies, which made excellent lamps when caught in suffi-cient number, roly-polies were my childhood bug of choice. They not only allowed themselves to be captured without any mess or fuss, but they also fit quite nicely into the plastic Coates & Clark zipper con-tainers I found in the sewing box in my mother's room. When not in use as tables in my apple-crate dollhouse, those little plastic capsules made great terrariums for the unlucky pillbugs I plucked from the edge of the lawn.

What I didn't know then, of course, was just how out of place the creatures really are. Cousin to a host of species known as woodlice, some of which have adapted to land more fully than others, pillbugs seem to spend their entire lives seeking just the right level of mois-ture. Their chitinous shells notwithstanding, they quickly lose water through evaporation and excretion, water that must be replaced somehow.

They've managed to live with this liability only because of certain instinctive behaviors—specifically, their tendency to avoid sunlight and to congregate in dark, moist places, such as the undersides of rocks and logs. Pressing themselves against the damp surface of the earth, or the body of another pillbug, the creatures in effect evade the risk of drying up.

Not surprisingly, it's also moisture that draws them out of hibernation in the spring.

"The snail and pillbug population is exploding," a friend writes after a recent heavy rain, "and I'm thinking of nixing the organic stuff for one good treatment of whatever will hold them at bay. They do love my beans."

Omnivores, pillbugs love not only my friend's green beans but also her grass clippings and her leaves, the rotten fruits and vegetables she throws in her compost bin, the remains of any animals that happen to wander into her garden to die.

Useful as they are as scavengers, pillbugs can nonetheless wear out their welcome fast—particularly as their numbers begin to soar. Depending on the location, a female may well produce two broods in a single year, with each brood ranging from roughly thirty to eighty newborns. Carrying her eggs in a brood pouch or marsupium on her underside, the pillbug releases her young after a period of about two months. At that point, the infant pillbugs simply climb down the first of their mother's fourteen legs and head off for a life of roly-poly bliss on their own.

And for *Armadillidium vulgare*, that life may be long indeed—at least compared to the ordinary garden pest's. On average, a pillbug will survive for about two years, although some have lived for as long as five.

So who's to know, then, if the pillbugs on my porch in June are not the ones I swept off last July? Or if those that last week feasted on the remnants of a possum on the backyard path were not, two years before, digesting lettuce in my compost bin?

Small world, I am tempted to say. But instead I merely brush them out of the way, letting them get on with their business, letting them get on with the task of recycling the world.

Seeing the World
Up Close

L ISTENING TO THE WHIR of my tires on the hot asphalt and
the light breeze rustling through the corn, I think of my
friend who has recently moved to Nevada. Three weeks after
packing everything he owned and heading west in a rental truck, he
wrote to tell me of his trip.

"The subtle shifts in climate, vegetation, and even soil color," he
said, "are perceptible from the road in a way, of course, that travel
from the air completely obscures."

I think of his words because, for the first time ever, I am seeing this
landscape up close. Minus the roar of an engine, the barrier of a
windshield, the blast of icy air against my skin, I am coming to know
this place in a whole new way.

It was just after 7:00 A.M. when two friends and I strapped on our
helmets, climbed on our bicycles, and headed south down an unpaved
county road. "So far, so good," one of them had said when we
stopped for a drink and a look at where we were. At that point, the
sun had just cleared the crest of a hay field, suffusing the air with a
golden glow.

Where has this been? I wondered, awed not just by the open space but
by the sheer fact of the sun. *Where are all the mornings that I've missed?*

Unaccustomed as I am to being out at this hour—outside my
house, my office, my car—I sensed that the world had reformed itself

in my absence, that the whole of it had been reborn not just once but a million times, and all without my knowing.

So how do we know the earth? That is the question that greets me this morning as I coast down a gravel road, as I laugh with the wind in my face, as I sit at a highway rest stop rich with swallows. Is it enough simply to show up?

Perched on a bicycle seat that feels far too small and far too hard for my middle-aged frame, I pedal as fast as I can. Legs, arms, back—surprisingly, each potential weak spot, each unprepared part of my self, is holding up fine so far.

The route my friends and I have chosen this morning—or, rather, the route we'll make up as we go—will take us through twenty-six miles of southern Blackland Prairie. Stretching from the Red River down to San Antonio, this four-hundred-mile-long "horn of plenty," as some have called it, comprises much of the state's best farmland.

In the words of Richard Phelan, author of *Texas Wild,* "The land lies in smooth, rolling hills, like enormous green waves, their crests a mile or more apart, the curves interlocking. The long bowed lines that airplanes draw in the sky match exactly the lines of the hills. The valleys, where they exist, are as shallow as saucers, miles across, rich, and immensely calm."

Lying as it does just below the Balcones Escarpment, this northern edge of the Gulf Coastal Plain once sat at the bottom of a Cretaceous sea. Some seventy million years later, on his 1854 expedition through Texas, W. B. Parker described it as a sea of a different sort. "Below," he wrote in *Notes Taken during the Expedition Commanded by Capt. R. B. Marcy,* "lay a sea of pale green, flowers of every variety, shade, and form interspersed over the surface; a dark green belt of verdure here and there marking the ravines and watercourses, scattered in such perfect arrangement over the whole, as to seem as though some eminent artist had perfected the work."

Now a patchwork quilt of fields, this is a land of cotton and corn and hay, a land of hackberry and mesquite, and, nearer the river bottoms, cottonwood and pecan. This is a land, too, of scissortails sitting on fences, of mourning doves flushed from the road, of solitary larks.

Would I have seen these riches from my car? Perhaps. But as John Daniel admits in "The Impoverishment of Sightseeing," the experience just isn't the same.

Recalling a trip to Yosemite, the first he had taken in years, Daniel describes the feelings he had while touring the park in a bus. "We thought the bus would give us many good views, and it did," he writes. "But how disappointing those views were, how unaccountably dull."

The reason? "The places that had once been alive to me, imbued with my zeal and fears," Daniel says, "now were reduced to plain visual images, seen for the sake of seeing, scenes in the bus window."

How can I best know the earth? How can I know my own life?

Flying down a hill on a summer morning, I don't think of myself as a middle-aged woman whose survival rides on two thin tires, a plastic helmet, and the courtesy of drivers I don't know. Oddly enough, flying down a hill on a sun-drenched country road, I don't think of myself at all.

What I do think about, I realize, is how a corn husk shimmers like a snake as it blows across the road, how a redwing blackbird's song floats up invisibly from a field, how, as day wears on, shade shrinks, compresses, disappears.

This, I tell myself, is why I'm here—this heat, this musky scent of hay, this wind against my gritty skin, this joy.

Immediate and clean, the morning wraps itself around me like the air. Up ahead, my friend is scouting for a final patch of shade. I pedal on.

In the Toyah Valley

I T IS HARDLY the valley of my dreams.

Dotted with soaptree yucca and creosote bush, the sandy soil rolls on for miles. Just as it tends to do in any desert landscape, life in this arid place recedes, waits, hides in shadows cast by rocks and clumps of thorny scrub. In the heat of the midday sun, only a burrowing owl has chosen to show itself. Almost invisible against the tawny earth, the bird sits motionless and mute atop a metal post.

A mile or so away, a yellow highway sign incongruously warns: "Watch for Water on the Road." Some witty person's idea of a joke? A flood here in the desert? But then we spot a second sign just like it and realize that the cautionary words are on the up and up. The rain, when it comes, isn't channeled away but spreads, covering this desiccated land like glass.

What we're driving through, I later learn, is a basin formed by eons of decay. Borne by wind and rain, pieces of the mountains to the west have worn away, dissolved, deposited themselves as sand and gravel here upon this sun-baked plain. It is the quintessential wasteland, unforgiving, hard.

As we make our way along this two-lane county road, I check the map and figure that the basin's lowest point is roughly five miles to our east at a spot called Toyah Lake. Bisected by U.S. Highway 285, where it runs between the West Texas towns of Fort Stockton and Pecos, Toyah Lake is in reality a playa, a shallow, alkaline basin stretched between outcroppings of Cretaceous limestone and ridges of Triassic shales and sandstones.

"In Spanish," Eric Bolen writes in the *Handbook of Texas*, "playa means 'beach,' and the word was perhaps chosen because the lakes represent essentially all of the naturally occurring surface water in a vast semiarid region—the 'only beach in town.'" Looking out across the sand, I find his explanation apt.

Still, the name of this place seems to be an exercise in irony. Toyah, I've discovered, is a Jumano Indian word meaning "floating water" or "much water." Another satiric twist? Not at all. Though this alluvial plain is a dry, windblown flat for much of the year, when sudden rainstorms come, it does in fact become a lake. Running in from Salt Draw to the west and Toyah Creek to the east, water covers the caliche-crusted earth for up to ten square miles—less surface area than the average Texas playa, but large enough to merit mention on the map.

"Hard to imagine," I tell my husband as I scan the horizon for clouds. Ahead of us, a small dust devil dances on the shoulder of the road. It is the only movement visible for miles.

Driving north from Balmorhea, we are headed not for the lake but for the community of Toyah, once a busy hub of transportation, now a town where empty buildings seem the norm. "Cross the railroad tracks, turn right, then left on DuBois Street," our guidebook tells us. "Remain on DuBois to Fourth Street. Turn left."

Zigzagging through the little town, we pause just long enough to wonder how the life was wrung from it, and when. The two-story red brick bank, its portico supported by a rank of tall white pillars; the two-story mercantile, the words *corn* and *hay* just barely visible on one wall; the turn-of-the-century school—all these buildings, and more, are boarded up, abandoned, remnants of a long gone past.

According to Julia Cauble Smith, also in the *Handbook of Texas*, Toyah had its beginnings as a trading post for area ranchers. Shortly thereafter—in 1881, to be precise—the Texas and Pacific Railroad came in, making the town its stopping point between Sweetwater and El Paso. "By October 20, 1881," Smith notes, "Toyah was described as a town of tents, saloons, and restaurants. At the end of the year the Overland Transportation Company announced stagecoach service from Toyah to Fort Stockton and Fort Davis—six times each way weekly."

Ultimately, Toyah became a hub for cattle shipments too, and between 1914 and 1929, its population remained stable at just over one thousand. But with the decision to make nearby Toyahvale the new point of departure for shipping livestock, Toyah began to decline. As of 1990, its population was a mere 115.

But it's not the town itself that brings us here today. It's the rocks. For the second day in a row, my husband and I have grabbed our hats, left the morning chill of the Davis Mountains, and made our way down to the hot and dusty flats below. Rock hammer and guidebook in hand, we have lost track of the hours as we've wandered, eyes on the ground, through fields of West Texas stone.

As we drive through the town of Toyah, I double-check the directions in my *Rockhound's Guide to Texas*. Once we take a left on Fourth, I read, we're to follow an unmarked county road to the west. We're likely to have good luck, writer Melinda Crow tells us, in "any rocky area, for about seven miles."

What intrigues me even more than this, however, is Crow's description of the rocks it's possible to find there. "Agate of every imaginable color can be found around the tiny town," Crow writes. "The most prized pieces are those of a blue plume, which is so dark it appears black in the harsh West Texas sun."

"Where do we start?" I ask my husband when we finally stop. In front of us, there is rock as far as we can see. Gravel in its natural state.

Myriad shades of green, pink, white, blue, red—the colors are too numerous to name. Is it the sun or my surprise that makes me dizzy with delight? Is it the heat reflecting off the asphalt or the sight of so much treasure lying right here on the ground that keeps me anchored to this spot?

No matter. There are wonders here indeed, original earth, mountains I can pick up, hold, hide in the palm of my hand. We start to dig.

Homecoming

THEY HAVE BEEN on my desk for weeks now, arranged like miniature apples in a small ceramic bowl.

"Shouldn't you move them?" my husband asked when, thinking them beautiful, I left them on the table in the hall. "The cleaning woman's coming tomorrow, and she might think they're candy."

I had serious doubts that she would, I told him, but I moved them just the same. And here they continue to sit, seven tiny wren eggs, perfectly made, intact.

What a waste, I had thought as I slipped the gourd house from its stubby branch, as I carried it to a nearby bench, as I pulled its contents, stick by stick, out through the narrow hole. Six weeks before, I had watched a pair of Bewick's wrens construct the twiggy nest, and I had watched as, day after day, a female cowbird had kept them from it, gradually driving the wrens away.

Abandoned, the house had been quiet for weeks. A titmouse had peered in once or twice, as had a pair of Carolina wrens, but finding the gourd house full, each of them had flown away at once.

Ultimately, I resolved to clean it out, to make a space for whatever might show up next. Past the brittle twigs, past the shreds of ball moss and cellophane and feathers from our ringneck doves, past the turquoise dryer lint I'd left hanging on a limb last March—past all of these things and more lay the clutch of seven speckled eggs, small as thumbnails, and as slick.

How delicate, I thought as each one rolled into my open palm, how improbable and fine.

Sitting at my desk now, I light a candle and hold each of the eggs, in turn, up to the flame. What do I expect to see? Feathers, bones, blood, the outline of an infant wren? Or am I looking for something else—the answer to a question, perhaps, some missing fragment of my life?

Holding a single wren egg in my hand, letting it rest in the crevice where my fingers meet my palm, I imagine the trill of a tiny bird, its feathers fluffed and weightless in the wind. I imagine a life that isn't mine, a life both larger and smaller than my own.

The luminous life of the world.

More and more, I realize, I turn to this natural world not just for beauty and solace, not just for pleasure and peace, but for the wisdom that I need to live. It teaches me things in a language I can hear and understand.

On the corner of my desk at the university where I teach sits the shell of a red-eared slider, a gift from a friend who found it on the river bank south of town. For my students, I'm sure that the message it sends is mixed:

Here is a woman who keeps dead turtles on her desk.

Beware.

Or

Here is a woman who knows how to love the world.

Come in.

I can see the words reflected in their eyes.

If the foot-long turtle shell doesn't scare them away, or at least keep them cowering at the door, these students eventually scan the room for other clues to who I am. They see the upper half of a possum skull perched matter-of-factly on the computer behind my desk. They see three red maple leaves, sent one autumn by a friend who was traveling through Maine. Chunks of obsidian and banded rhyolite, bits of copper ore, flight feathers and iridescent tail feathers from a Rio Grande turkey, butterfly wings, an acorn from a large bur oak, a piece of Japanese cedar from a friend in Tokyo, a cicada, pinyon pine leaves in a little bowl, the first cardinal feather of the season, found by a friend in her garden—like the wrens that built their nest outside my window in March, I am building a nest as well. Sheltered by bits and pieces of the world, I am nurtured by a host of other lives.

Sitting in my study, a single wren egg in my hand, I am torn by the inclinations of my head and heart. Part of me wants simply to hold the thing, to feel its cool, hard shell against my open palm. Another part insists on knowing what it means.

Imagining these eggs beneath the warm, soft underbelly of a wren, I imagine, too, how she must feel. Instinctively, she has chosen to make herself at home in a world of sense. Instinctively, she has given birth to a life she can't begin to name. She has no words for such things, but she knows when that life needs tending, and she knows when she needs to move on.

Her body tells her what her mind cannot.

My body knows this life as well—in the sight of giant swallowtails dancing their double helix in the sun, in the scent of rosemary brushed against my flesh, in the sound of my husband's breathing as he sleeps.

Come in, this life urges in a million different ways. Humming in the wasp nest on my porch or glowing in the moonlight of an early summer night, it tells me what the wren intuits in the hollow of her bones.

Come in, it tells me. You are home.

Beauty in the Sandhills

RIVING SOUTH from Midland, Texas, to Odessa, I couldn't imagine a landscape more desolate than this. Along the highway, where empty buildings testified to the 1980s oil bust, clumps of grass erupted from cracks in asphalt parking lots; rusty pipe lay stacked behind lines of chain-link fence. Fences—they seemed strangely out of place there, out of place where there was no one to be kept out, and little to be kept in. Beyond the empty buildings, oil pumps stood like sun-dazed cattle, waiting for a sign to put them in motion again, a sign that might come soon or not at all.

It was strange, my daughter said from the back seat, strange that two cities of this size should be so empty. It was as if they had been built in some more hospitable place, only to be condemned by an evil wizard and moved here as punishment. I laughed at her theory, but in all honesty, it seemed as reasonable as the truth—that people would come here of their own free will.

And where, I wondered, were those people now? Resting in their air-conditioned living rooms? Watering their lawns? Hiding from the glare of the harsh West Texas sun? I could only imagine.

We had come to Midland for a family wedding. It was a happy occasion, a time for celebration and laughter. But the landscape—that was another matter indeed. Certain that we would find nothing beautiful there, we had dared it to prove us wrong.

And so it was with skepticism that we left our deserted motel and headed out along Interstate 20, the highway that runs from Midland to Odessa, to Pecos and into the desert Southwest. Our destination that day was the tiny town of Monahans, some fifty miles down the road.

"Why do we have to go there?" our daughter whined from the back seat. Now that her Walkman had died, she had suddenly realized where we were. And to a twelve-year-old, where we were was hardly promising.

Surprisingly, though, it was still cool when we reached Monahans Sandhills State Park, just five miles northeast of town. In front of the park headquarters, a ranger was lecturing a group of high school students, identifying for them the trees and shrubs that grew near the parking lot. Inside, a handful of tourists wandered through the air-conditioned museum, studying the displays of West Texas wildlife and artifacts.

Like the fences that guarded the empty buildings on the interstate, this phenomenon of nature seemed similarly out of place. Miles and miles of fine white sand, swirling into drifts along the road, banking itself into dunes—this was hardly what we'd come expecting to find.

Once covered by a Permian sea, this park is only a dot in the vast stretch of sand that runs for more than a hundred miles, blanketing five West Texas counties. Years of wind erosion created this sand, burning million-year-old sandstone into glistening grains of quartz. And even now, after a thousand years of shifting, these dunes still recreate themselves each day.

It would have been easy for us to assume that there was no life among the dunes, that these sandhills were as empty as the highway we'd just left. But here, on a path that cut through feathery gray wormwood and a patch of yellow primrose, was the side-winding trail of a desert snake, the nest of a packrat, the sound of a rabbit stirring in the brush. There were orioles and shrikes, and the raucous calls of crows.

Surprisingly, there was also good water just beneath the sand, water that once enticed Indians, Spanish explorers, and homesteaders to stop here on their journeys west. North of the park at Willow Springs, travelers found water particularly accessible, and it was here in 1883 that an entire wagon train of settlers was attacked and left for dead, presumably by the Comanches who used this watering hole as well.

So deep was the sand, however, that nearly twenty years would pass before anyone learned of these deaths. More precisely, it was in 1901 when the remains of forty burned wagons, human bones, and a collection of frontier artifacts were pulled from the dunes, revealing the violence that had occurred so many years before.

Today there are no wagon trains, no wolves, no Comanche raiders riding south toward Mexico and sweeping through this 3,840-acre park. But there are foxes and coyotes, jackrabbits and skunks, and flora unlike anything else in the state.

Just consider the Havard oaks.

Pausing on a trail behind the ranger station, visitors find it hard to believe that they are standing in the midst of a forest, one of the largest oak forests in North America. The scrubby trees that cover these dunes—and no, they are not dwarfed or stunted—are Havard shin oaks, a species that rarely exceeds three feet in height. In spite of their size, though, these little trees can send their roots to a depth of ninety feet, producing large acorns that are food for quail, javelina, and white-tailed deer.

I, for one, had suspected that by the end of my day at Monahans Sandhills State Park, I would be eager to return to the Texas Hill Country where I live, to a landscape more hospitable than this. But in these dunes and wildflowers and these clumps of yucca and grass, I had found a kind of life I hadn't counted on at all. I had found a rare sort of loveliness. I had found the beauty of the dunes.

Autumn Currents

I T IS 3:15 on an autumn afternoon and I am sitting on the bank of
the Guadalupe River just outside the little Texas town of Hunt.
Wedged between the roots of a great pecan tree, my back against
its rough trunk, I draw my knees up toward my chest and balance an
open book against the slope of my blue-jeaned thighs.

Reading with pen in hand, I stop to underline the words of Kathleen Norris, author of *Dakota: A Spiritual Geography*. "I prize the hiddenness of Dakota," she writes, "and have grown protective of the silence
here—the places that have become sacred to me, that in all likelihood
few humans have ever walked."

Red and near red, yellow gold on gold—far from the Great Plains
of Norris's Dakota, this stretch of Texas river wears the brilliance of
the fall's first chill. Above me, the leaves of the bald cypress, already
bronze and looking delicate as fennel, repeat themselves in the still,
green waters of the Guadalupe. At my feet, white thoroughwort spills
across the broken path, drawing yellow butterflies to itself like sunlight on water.

Eupatorium havanense—the name is lyrical, liquid on the tongue of
the imagination.

Far from the scoured landscape of Dakota, this river, this sky, this
afternoon wash over me as silence, unbroken save for the cry of a
single jay.

Impulsively, I lay my book aside and reach for the empty shell of a pecan that has fallen near my foot. Rough to the touch, it is a piece of earth returning to itself, matter becoming matter yet again.

"Beauty," says the poet Wallace Stevens, "is momentary in the mind—/ The fitful tracing of a portal: / But in the flesh it is immortal." How ironic, I tell myself, tracing the shell's sharp edges with my thumb. How disappointing that I would come to this place seeking solitude, finding loneliness instead. Is it the beauty of this perfect afternoon that pains me? The immensity of sky that weighs me down? Or is it that this moment goes unshared, unspoken, mysteriously unlived?

Farther down the bank, three women sit sunning themselves on a wooden swimming dock. Casually, one of them picks up a small stone and sends it arcing over the water. With the sound of its splash, circle echoes circle, moving gently toward the river's other edge.

As usual, I want to make something of this moment, but meaning can't be willed. All I can do, it seems, is pay attention, and so I begin an inventory of the world: cypress leaves arranged just so on limestone, a red-bellied woodpecker's call, Johnson grass luxuriantly gone to seed, sun on a turtle's back.

That I can note these things is evidence of their distance, evidence of the open space between the observer and observed. Conscious of their shape, their density, their size, I am conscious of my human boundaries as well.

Downstream, voices rise and fall on the gentle current of the wind. "I'm going in," one of the women says, dropping her shorts and shirt on the wooden dock. There is a splash, and then another and another. Laughter follows, filling the corridor of river with its golden sound.

I am envious of such joy.

"There's something liberating about leaving your clothes on the side," the swimmer calls out to the others. Turning away from the dock, she heads for sun-warmed water just beyond the trees.

And I, braced against the trunk of this pecan, consider the weight of the self out of water, consider its need to be borne on currents not its own.

"Ring around the rosies, pockets full of posies. Ashes, ashes, we all fall down." Holding hands and singing, submerged up to their shoulders, the three women circle in green water, heads held back to skim the surface of the river.

Listening to the song of these swimmers on a sunny afternoon, I imagine how such lightness would feel, how such a letting go might lift a heavy spirit turned without forgiveness on itself. Leaning into the curve of the tree, I imagine the mercy of the world consoling and supporting me. I imagine the river, and me in it, and the water bearing me away on a current of sweet, unfathomable peace.

Taking the Pulse
of the Earth

WATCHING THE WORLD come back to life?" my neighbor asks as he walks by one late January afternoon. I am caught. Pulling henbit and grass as fine as baby's hair from the flowerbed, I look up, smile, and give him a cursory wave.

"Checking the wildflowers," I acknowledge, the way one might profess to be going out to get the mail or put the trash can on the curb. Just another domestic chore, or so I make it sound.

In truth, however, I am taking the pulse of the earth.

Not lingering to talk, my neighbor moves on past the end of the split-rail fence, past the tangled clump of snakewood growing near the asphalt road. Even before he disappears, though, I have my fingers back in the dirt, back against the spindly shoots of larkspur and horsemint, greenthread and phlox.

Smelling like pepper after the midday rain, the soil is friable and dark, just the right consistency to let the roots of winter grass slip smoothly from the ground. They are cool against my fingertips, cool and damp as I release them, letting them fall to the earth as gift.

Three weeks ago, ice; today, this—this scent of winter honeysuckle, this sun against my face, this hint of green.

That's the way things go here in Central Texas. One day we are walking gingerly on the ice; the next, we are sure that spring has come. Season segues into season, all right, but not before doubling back on itself at least a time or two. False winter, false spring—living in the ambiguity of neither this nor that, we take our cues from the birds, from the trees, from our own brittle joints. Gradually, we learn that all predictions are subject to change. We keep a sweater handy just in case. We bring in plants.

For at least a week now, yet another pair of Bewick's wrens has been building a nest in the hollow gourd out front. Leaning forward ever so slightly at my desk, I have a clear view of the tree limb where their small house hangs. In and out, in and out they fly, bringing back twigs and leaves and slivers of grass, whatever has caught the attention of their tiny eyes.

Eventually, of course, I will have to look. Peering in while they are gone, I will see a nearly solid mass of white—fur, perhaps, or feathers from our pair of ringneck doves. Crisscrossed with broken twigs, the nest will at this point be missing just one thing—the clutch of eggs that would tell me this is more than a practice run.

Spring, and not-yet-spring; life, and not-yet-life. In a few days, a norther sliding down from Canada will remind me that spring is, in reality, more than a month away.

Later, as I lead a writing workshop on a crisp February morning, I will offer my students a question as audacious as the day. Where, I will ask them, do you meet Mystery in your life? Looking at me for just a moment—in puzzlement, no doubt—most will grip their pens and begin to write. Others will simply sit in silence, thinking—I imagine—or savoring the absence of thought.

"I need to go somewhere," a friend will tell me afterward, "maybe on a camping trip. Not far," she will add, "but somewhere."

Where do you meet Mystery in your life? Not in her middle class neighborhood, my friend will argue; not in the well-tended, tidy lawns; not in the glare of streetlights obscuring her view of the sky; not in anything familiar, expected, set.

That same afternoon, the words of my friend still echoing in my head, I will put on my jeans and a T-shirt, grab a saw from the back-yard shed, and begin the work of cutting down a tree.

Nearly killed by a fungus early in its eighteen years of life, this peppermint peach had grown not straight and tall but as a multi-trunked tree, expanding an inch in width for every inch in height. Gaudy in pinks and reds and white in the early spring, it had truly been a wonder in its prime. But now, gray with age, it blooms sparsely, if at all. Its time has clearly come.

Drawing the saw again and again across the smallest of its many trunks, I will cut deeply into the living wood. Surprised by its pinkness, by its freshness, by its scent, I will stand there for a moment before continuing, will slide my hand, at last, across the cracked and peeling bark.

"I'd like to leave it," I will say to my husband when the two of us have pruned the tree down to a single trunk. "I'd like to see just what it does."

Where do we meet Mystery in our lives? Could it be, perhaps, in the unpredictability of a Central Texas spring? In the wisdom of birds? In the fresh, pink heartwood of a tree?

Perhaps.

A December Walk
in the Woods

THEY MAKE GREAT SHADE," one of the women says, shielding her eyes from the sun. As she speaks, a narrow line of shadow covers her feet and spills itself like ink across the nubby asphalt road. Black vultures, floating high above us in the afternoon sky, have left their mark, their wings a temporary canopy above our heads.

With the rest of the group lagging far behind on the trail through Ottine Swamp, the three of us are dawdling now, are picking up odd bits of the forest as we walk. Turning to the young woman who has spoken, I notice that she is holding an enormous sycamore leaf, fan-like, against her open palm. It more than covers her slender hand.

We are like children, I suddenly realize, like first graders on a field trip through the autumn woods. And the world, luminous and crisp, lies just beneath our feet.

I have come here today, to Palmetto State Park, at the invitation of a friend. It is the last scheduled meeting of his graduate nature writing class, and he sensed that I'd want to tag along.

My friend was right.

Years ago, when my daughter was still an infant, this was the place I would come when I needed to escape. Grabbing my binoculars and the Peterson's field guide I had given my husband as a gift the Christmas before, I would drop her off at the babysitter's house, point the car south, and drive. Thirty minutes later, with the stresses of teaching and new motherhood feeling very far away, I'd be crouched at the edge of a slough, watching a pair of yellow-throats flitting through the reedy grass.

It was a way of staying sane.

Over time, my husband, my daughter, and I would return to Palmetto again and again. Walking through the swamp, or following the river trail through stands of bur and Durand oak, we would listen for the calls of the chickadees and titmice, would stand there in that canopy of trees and, with a toddler tugging at our pants, make check marks on our "life list" in the front of the Peterson guide: Ladder-backed woodpecker. Solitary vireo. Blackburnian warbler. Red-breasted nuthatch. One by one, we would check the blank before each name. One by one, we would learn the parts of the world.

Today, as I drove the narrow park road blanketed with leaves, I thought of those bird-watching Sunday afternoons, of the flickers barking their loud *klee-yer*, of the fox that once had dashed in front of us on this very stretch of road. And somehow, this memory connected me, placed me firmly in the present. "X," it told me. "You are here."

Where I am, I should add, is a place that is out of place. "It resembles a patch of exuberant jungle, escaped from the tropics and surrounded by austere Post Oak country," Richard Phelan writes in *Texas Wild*. "Dwarf palmettos grow fiercely here, far from the Gulf Coast riverbottoms which are their natural range. The park is named for them."

Created in 1936, Palmetto has the look of all CCC-era parks—the big stone pavilion, the stone culverts on the narrow road, the stone retaining wall high above the river. An almost rusty maroon, these smooth, round stones—like the palmettos themselves—seem strangely foreign. And yet, they are part of my memory too.

After sharing a potluck lunch, an assortment of breads and meats and salads appearing from the back seats of our cars, we head en masse toward the trailhead just down the road. Here on a Tuesday afternoon, less than three weeks from the winter solstice, the eleven of us—my friend and I, his seven students, a recent graduate, and another colleague—have these roughly 268 acres to ourselves. Nonetheless, we saunter down the Palmetto Trail as a group, stopping to listen as my friend reads the guide he picked up at the trailhead near the road.

Hailing as they do from other parts of the country, many of the students find the plant life here, more than five hundred species in all, to be mysterious and new. They watch, enthralled, as their teacher points out first a bur oak, then a bois d'arc, then a cedar elm.

"Is this dead?" asks a woman from New York state. What she has pointed to, I realize, is a red buckeye, an especially nice understory plant that seems to spend most of its life in dormancy. Losing its leaves in the heat of summer, it appears to be dead for a good eight months, until its tubular red flowers and slender leaves reappear in early spring.

Toward the end of the trail, two of the faster walkers and I stop to study the pumphouse tower built at the edge of the swamp. On one side of the structure is a locked door; on the other, a Plexiglas-covered commentary on the park's artesian springs.

Had we arrived a few decades earlier—say, before the 1970s—we might have seen more than the sulfurous pools of water we find here today. Thanks to Palmetto's odd geology, we might also have seen mud bubbling up from one of the park's active mud volcanoes—some as large as thirty feet across and five feet high—or from their smaller counterparts known as "mud boils."

Explaining this strange phenomenon, Richard Phelan notes that the land beneath the swamp is riddled with cracks, all of which allow trapped water and gas to escape.

Of all the facts we learn about the park, however, none is more remarkable than the diversity of life that exists here, an ecological richness exceeded in Texas only by the wetlands along the coast and the lower Rio Grande.

Indeed, were we a quieter group, we would no doubt be seeing more of the estimated 239 bird species known to inhabit this park. As it is, we have spotted only the occasional cardinal, the band of twittering titmice, the knot of high-flying vultures scouting the ground for food.

Reaching the edge of the road, one of my two walking companions veers off to enjoy a moment alone. Turning to the other, a writer in her twenties, I recall that she is a spelunker, which has strongly influenced her work.

"It's difficult to write about caves," she tells me. "There's nothing there to see, nothing much to be described."

I think of her words later on, when the others are gone and I am alone in the park. Sitting on the low stone wall above the river, my journal lying open in my lap, I listen to the riffling of the water below, and catch the bantering of titmice—*peter, peter, peter*—coming from the trees at my back.

How do I write about this, I wonder, about a moment in the woods when the sky is a seamless blue, and the cottonwoods shiver, and the earth is all spent leaves? How do I speak of the ladder-backed woodpecker whose *pick-pick-pick* invites me down a forest trail, deeper and deeper toward the center of a shady autumn wood? And how do I write of that place inside myself, when I arrive, that place as silent as any cave, as full of mystery, as destitute of sense?

Sliding off my rocky perch, I head for a tree I have noticed in the thicket at my left. A dark but brilliant red, the leaves of the rusty blackhaw shimmer in the waning light. I retrieve one from the ground, slide it carefully between the pages of my journal, and wind the leather binding shut. For now, it will be the only record of this day.

And it will be enough.

To Be at Home

D o you feel it? Doesn't it feel different than home?"

"Yeah," the young boy tells his father, "it feels a lot different than inside the house."

"No," the father says, his voice charged with excitement, "I mean different from the outside of the house, too. Do you feel the energy? There's a lot of energy here."

Perched on the side of the hill, just out of their line of sight, I can imagine the father pressing his open palm against the rock and looking deep into the little boy's eyes, the two of them connecting with the primal, ancient pulse that surges through the earth.

How would they feel to know that I, a stranger, was sharing this moment with them?

I should feel guilty, I suppose, but eavesdropping was never my intent. "You go ahead," I had told my students Biss and Jen when we came to this part of the hike. "I'll be fine right here."

Handing my backpack and camera to Biss, I watched as the two young people scrambled up the wall of rock behind me. Blessed with a bad right knee, a fear of heights, and a singularly poor sense of balance, I had resigned myself to doing what I've done so many times before: staying behind while others, more sure-footed and confident than I, went on to see what beauties lay at the other end of the trail.

In this case, we all knew, it would be a splendid sunset, made all the more delicious by the view from the top of Little Rock.

With my students gone, and the father and son too far away to hear now, I console myself with the sight of the lucent, ample moon. Nearly full, it rests above a line of live oaks to the east. I lie against the rocks and watch it rise. Round and white, it is a portal in the still-blue evening sky. If I squint my eyes just right, I can imagine that I am looking up the neck of a bottle, looking into the universe, waiting to feel myself poured out into a vast and silent space.

"Do you feel it? Doesn't it feel different than home?" Perhaps that father was right. Perhaps these rocks do contain an energy that can move us to visions, or pronouncements, or at least to a clearer sense of who and where we are.

Located just north of Fredericksburg on the Llano Uplift of Texas, Little Rock is only one among a string of Precambrian granite domes comprising Enchanted Rock State Natural Area. Originally they were all part of a single batholith, a single formation of igneous rock, but thanks to weathering and erosion, the granite has broken along its fracture zones to create several distinctly separate domes.

The largest of these, Enchanted Rock, stands 445 feet above the surrounding countryside. In the parlance of geologists, it is an exfoliation dome—that is, a large mass from which sheets of rock have been peeled away, reducing the external pressure on the dome and allowing the rock once buried far beneath the surface to rise even farther to the top. Like the tip of an iceberg, Enchanted Rock is but a tiny fraction of the tons of molten rock that flowed up through the surrounding Packsaddle schist a billion years ago. The bulk of its granite mass has yet to be exposed.

At an elevation of 1,825 feet, Enchanted Rock has long been a source of curiosity and wonder. "Indians, not real-estate men, gave the rock its name," Richard Phelan writes in *Texas Wild*. "They believed it was enchanted, that spirits lived on its top. From nearby camps they saw strange glimmers of 'spirit fire' at night, and heard mysterious noises coming from the rock. Some Indians would climb up it—in daylight—to leave offerings. Others feared the spirits and would not touch even the base of the rock. When white men first came, they found well-worn trails leading up to the rock from all around the horizon. It was a major place of worship."

How to explain the eerie sights and sounds emanating from these rocks? The most logical theory is that the mysterious glow seen at sunset and dawn is caused by light glinting off feldspar crystals embedded in the granite dome. Similarly, the otherworldly noises are probably nothing more than the product of expanding and contracting rock.

"Do you feel the energy? There's a lot of energy here." Does knowing how such a source of wonder came to be detract from its mystery and power? For me, the answer is no.

Recalling his first ascent of Guadalupe Peak, environmental historian Dan Flores writes in *Horizontal Yellow:* "Some ancient impulse gave me to understand even then that if you seek the power of a place, climbing some protruding piece of its vertical geometry can lay open rhythms not discernible from the lowlands, the visual equivalent of placing an ear to a seashell."

Poised on the eastern face of Little Rock, with the chill of evening falling fast against my skin, I note that a glow of lavender and gold has gathered low above the distant trees. Behind me, the voices of children echo through the billion-year-old rocks.

"Do you feel it? Doesn't it feel different than home?" Not at all, I want to tell that father and his son. Here on the Llano Uplift, here amid the ancient energies of rocks and moon and spirit fires burning in the dark, I am reminded again that there is just one home, one earth, one rhythm pulsing through it all.

Loss

Elegy for a Jay

I T APPEARS as a small flash of blue.

Jay, I think, the color catching somewhere in the corner of my eye.

A half mile down the road, I pull off, turn around, and drive to the spot where it lies. There, just barely on the pavement, is the body of a brilliantly colored bird.

Checking the traffic, I head for the shoulder and stop. One car whips past, then another right behind it, and then nothing for as far as I can see.

I know that I must be quick.

Picking up the bird, I am struck by how very light it is. As if hollow, or stuffed with bits of straw, it weighs little more than the air. It rests on my hand like a breath.

Having driven this route for roughly twenty years, I can imagine how the bird met its end. In my mind, I can see it swooping headlong out of the woods, can hear it calling to its mate somewhere across the road, can feel its final second of surprise.

Weighing between an eighth and a quarter of a pound, the jay would have died at once. A thump against the fender, a bump against the glass, it might as well have been a rock or a stick or an empty drink can lying in the road.

I suspect the driver never knew.

Placing the bird on the floorboard of my car, I notice the absence of blood. *Strange*, I think, considering the way that it died. Strange that there would be no feathers out of place, no wings askew, no mark of any kind. Strange that there would be just this: this unnatural tilt of the blue-crested head, this lack of light in the hard, unblinking eyes.

It is difficult, as I drive toward my house, not to wonder about what I've done. Granted, my husband and I have often stopped to look at ruined creatures lying lifeless by the road—the auburn body of a fox, the tawny nutria, the hawk that flew too low. More commonly, of course, we've simply driven on. Veering past the carnage, we've groaned at the sight of a family of raccoons run over in the night. We've winced at the fawn sprawled stiff-legged in the grass. We've grieved the turtle's lack of speed.

But we've never brought them home.

So why am I doing it now? Out of curiosity, in part, out of a simple desire to know. In short, I want to see this bird up close.

Unmistakable with its bright blue crest, its necklace of black, its barred wings and tail, and its sturdy-looking bill, the blue jay is easy enough to spot. A common resident of woodlands and gardens alike, this member of the *Corvidae* family shares many of the characteristics of its kin, the myriad crows and magpies of the world.

As Steve Madge and Hilary Burn explain in *Crows and Jays*, "Vocally they typically utter harsh squawks, croaks or screeching calls, but, despite this, many corvids have a remarkably varied vocabulary." Intelligent and curious birds, the corvids are bold as well, often to the point of aggression.

Once, I recall, when my husband and I were staying in a house at the foot of Colorado's Mount Yale, we were awakened each morning by a mob of angry jays. Accustomed to being fed on time, the Steller's jays and the gray jays, along with a Clark's nutcracker or two, would routinely peck on the windows and roof until we came outside with their seed.

Notorious for their alarm cries, which they use to announce the presence of owls and cats and even the people who feed them, blue jays, admittedly, are not always welcomed as guests. Some people would agree with Thoreau, who described their call as an "unrelenting steel-cold scream . . . unmelted, that never flows into a song, a sort of wintry trumpet, screaming cold; hard, tense, frozen music, like the winter sky itself."

It is not a view I share.

Brazen and raucous as they are, blue jays can also be quite shy. Indeed, at times it is only the rustle of leaves, the whisper of feathers on wind, the liquid *tull-ull, tull-ull* that gives the furtive birds away.

It is this melodic song I think of as I take the creature from my car. Stroking its sleek blue wings, running a finger backwards on its light gray breast, I imagine its last impression of the world, its keen desire, its eyes aglow with life.

When the time comes to bury the jay, I dig a hole beneath the Turk's cap near the deck, lay the bird carefully inside, then cover it with soil. It is a small ritual, no doubt, but it is a way of saying that this creature's life has somehow been a part of mine.

In his essay "Apologia," Barry Lopez reflects on his own habit of occasionally stopping and removing animals from the road. "Once a man asked, Why do you bother?" Lopez writes. "You never know, I said. The ones you give some semblance of burial, to whom you offer an apology, may have been like seers in a parallel culture. It is an act of respect, a technique of awareness."

It is, in a sense, all we have to give.

Earth to Earth

AFTER WEEKS of dutiful plodding, weeks of doing only what I've had to do, I feel the restlessness of early spring. Granted, it is winter still, and there is time for two or three more cold fronts to blow in. But the scent of native honeysuckle fills the sunny afternoon, and hyacinths explode in blooms of blue amid last autumn's leaves. Nearly lost beneath green sumac, purple and white anemones—windflowers—raise themselves on slender stems. Abandoned bird nests, awry and ragged in the tops of naked trees, remind me of another spring. Witnesses to birth and death and the weather of a Central Texas year, they are held in place by nothing more than gravity and air.

Whether it's the warm sun on my skin, or some genetic urge to rearrange my world, I find myself in search of something I can transplant, trim, remove. Craving order, I wander through the garden, snipping off the frozen tips of asters, pulling henbit from the lawn, cutting back the flame acanthus.

I would spend the day this way, provided that my back and shoulders tolerated the abuse. But since they don't, I leave the greater portion of the work for later on. Satisfied that I've done all the gardening I can, I gather up my tools and place them on the wooden bench that sits beside the front door of my house.

But I am restless still.

Moments later, I am out in the garage, considering the contents of a freezer left untended far too long. Badly in need of defrosting, it is filled with food gone bad, not months but years ago. I feel a twinge of guilt as I begin to pry the plastic packets from their shelves and drop them one by one into the trash.

The sausage that we never really liked, the freezer-burned ground beef, the bags of dried-out rolls—how was it that we let it go to waste?

And then I see the peas.

"Cooked cream peas for Susie," reads the handwritten note stapled to a Seal-a-Meal bag. "Remove staple before cooking." Noting that familiar backhand script, and those all too blunt instructions, I am jarred by a past that might have been twelve years ago or just last week.

I am jarred, quite simply, by a presence that has caught me by surprise.

"June 1992," reads the ink on the outside of a bag of okra. *What was I doing then?* I wonder. *Was this the year before my mother died?* How odd that memory would fail to recollect a date like that.

Dropping the bags of frozen vegetables and bread into a plastic tub, I take them to the compost pile where, carefully, I open them and pour their contents—sealed in ice—into the metal bin.

Earth to earth, I think, wondering if there will be a pea patch out here in the spring.

I wonder, too, about the pain that comes with letting go of things. There's still one package, for example—a rectangle of foil containing who knows what—that I cannot bring myself to throw away. Not yet, at least.

I'm not yet ready to give up this remnant of my mother's kitchen, her note of instruction taped across the plastic bag. I'm not yet ready to give up this meager scrap of nourishment, however cold and tasteless it may be.

Rational? Not in the least. Practical? Not by any standard that makes sense.

And yet, I would suggest, it's real—real as the messy edges of a winter trying to be spring, real as the desire to be done with what is dead.

Wild Things

I SAW SOMETHING WILD the other day—really wild.

Having let our yellow Lab outside to run around a while, I stood at the edge of the deck and watched as she explored the woods beside the house. Whether it was the sound she made rustling through the leaves or the sound that I made calling her back, I don't know. Either way, something was disturbed.

That something announced itself with a high, thin shriek, the shriek of a bird in distress. I immediately thought of the cats. Well fed as they may be, they still find pleasure in stalking the occasional bird. I scold them, they pout, and the bird—if it's lucky—flies away to sing another day.

But this was something far more primal than that, far more terrible and raw.

Appearing first as a blur at the edge of my field of sight, the stocky bird exploded from the woods, passed in front of me, and disappeared into another copse of trees. Hanging head-down from its claws was a male cardinal, still alive, its black eyes glimmering against the brilliant red.

I felt the breath catch in my throat.

To say that I'd never seen such a thing before would not be entirely true. Two summers ago, standing on a lakeshore in Montana, I watched in awe as an osprey hovered low above the water, dipped, and came up with a fish clamped tightly with its feet. I have seen the prey of "butcher birds" impaled on a barbed wire fence, the remains of mice, their bones stripped of flesh, regurgitated by an owl on the hunt late at night.

Though I've seen these things and never flinched, the plight of the cardinal gave me pause. Predator and prey—it's a symbiosis of the most primeval kind. It's how the world works. So why did I find this bird's impending death so hard to take?

Letting this question rest in the back of my mind, I began sorting out exactly what I'd seen. *Owl*, I had thought at first. Just weeks before, my husband and I had awakened from semisleep, put on our shoes, and gone out on the deck to listen to the *who cooks for you, who cooks for you all* of a barred owl.

Thinking that the sonorous call was coming from the trees behind our house, we sat there quietly in the dark, letting the sound enclose us like a mist. Finally, though, we realized that the bird was actually out front, perched in the top of a forty-foot Spanish oak. And so we carefully made our way around the house, getting as close as we dared to the tree, standing together in silence as the owl called once, then again, then flew.

Until that night, the only owls I had heard announcing their presence near our house were screech owls and the occasional great horned owl—the latter usually at some distance. But now, here was a barred owl, nearly as large as a great horned owl and every bit as loud.

It made me think first of owls when I saw that bird carrying its cardinal prey away. But this was no owl. While some owls, such as the burrowing owl, do hunt by day, I could tell at once that this was something else.

Hawk, I thought, suddenly wondering what a raptor—even such a small one as this—was doing in our woods. I found myself recalling a scene I'd come upon two springs before on a lonely South Texas road. Walking by a spot where I'd seen a great horned owl perching on a fence post the evening before, I noticed a drift of feathers in the grass.

Looking more closely, I spotted a single wing—gray, unblemished, soft and springy to the touch.

Remnant of a Cooper's hawk, the predator become prey.

Standing in my back yard, still taking in the drama I had seen, I realized that this scene, too, involved a Cooper's hawk.

Named in 1828 for New York naturalist William Cooper, the Cooper's hawk is one of the group of raptors known as bird hawks or, more colloquially, "chicken hawks." Like the goshawk and the sharp-shinned hawk, this accipiter is a long-tailed bird with short, rounded wings and a penchant for hunting in thickets and woods. Its favored prey consists of medium-sized songbirds like mourning doves and jays.

Slightly smaller than a crow, the Cooper's hawk can be recognized by its gray-blue back, streaked breast, and the highly visible black bands on the underside of its tail. Unlike that of buteos such as the soaring red-tailed and broad-winged hawks, the flight of the Cooper's hawk is described by Peterson as "several short beats and a glide." And indeed, that's precisely what I saw the day this creature swooped across our yard.

Known more for "ambushing" than for chasing prey, the Cooper's hawk was long hated for its habit of snatching poultry out of farm-yards. Violence against the bird, as well as a loss of habitat, led to a serious population decline beginning in the 1930s. Exacerbated by the use of DDT and other pesticides in the 1950s and 1960s, this decrease in population resulted in the Cooper's hawk being listed as endangered or threatened in many parts of the country, particularly in the east.

In recent years, though, the bird has made a comeback. According to George H. Harrison, writing for the National Wildlife Federation in 1997, both the Cooper's hawk and its slightly smaller counterpart the sharp-shinned hawk have recovered to such a degree that they are now frequently spotted hunting at backyard feeders.

"In one recent winter study," Harrison writes, "researchers at Cornell Laboratory of Ornithology reported that sharp-shinned hawks visited the yards of about 20 percent of the 8,000 people who record species at home for a program called Project FeederWatch. Cooper's hawks visited about 11 percent of the participants' yards. In all, hawks were responsible for 45 percent of the nearly 1,000 predator 'instances' at feeders in North America that were recorded in the 1993 study."

To some, Harrison admits, this resurgence of raptors comes as bad news. For others, it's a source of awe and delight. And for me? Watching that hawk disappear with the shrieking bird in its claws, I couldn't help but wonder if I'd seen that cardinal at my study window earlier in the day. Or if it was one of the several fledglings I'd watched grow from gawky infants to adept and agile adults.

Of course, I would never know.

"Nature, red in tooth and claw," said Alfred, Lord Tennyson. An unlikely source of poetry, it is nonetheless a source of mystery and life. A mind can feed for years on a paradox like this.

Tableau in the Grass

T HE BUTTERFLY WATCHING is beginning to pick up," a
friend remarked several days ago. "It's a great remedy for
overwhelm."

And so, with my friend's words fresh in my mind, I strolled
through my garden in the late afternoon, the knees of my jeans gold
with pollen, the back of my neck warm with sun.

Sure enough, I found, the butterflies were out. Drifting in from the
eastern corner of the yard, a giant swallowtail dipped and sailed,
dipped and sailed above the greenthread. More skittish, sulphurs
skimmed the tops of flowers like pebbles skipped across a lake. Only a
painted lady, tawny orange in the late day's light, lingered long enough
to feed.

Across the driveway, where the plants were more densely packed, I
had to push away a clump of horsemint growing in the path. And in
doing so, I was startled by a single butterfly pressed tightly to the back
of a vitex leaf.

Was it eating, I wondered? Laying eggs? Only when I bent down
closer, my eye just inches from the stem, was I aware of what was really
taking place. A tiny spider, four translucent legs around the butterfly
and four clamped firmly to the margins of the leaf, was readying a
feast.

Nudging the butterfly with my fingertip, I assumed that the creature was paralyzed, or if not that, just recently dead. Eyes black and

shiny in the sun, wings intact, proboscis out and curled as if in preparation for a drink, the insect hung in limbo, frozen in the final instant of its life.

Butterflies, for all their agility and grace, lead the most precarious of lives. As larvae, they fall prey to fire ants and fungi, parasites and birds. Offensive to scrupulous gardeners, they are plucked from their host plants, flung to the ground, and mashed. Some, no luckier than the rest, simply die for want of food.

Past the chrysalis stage, assuming that they live this long, butterflies can easily be drowned in a driving rain or killed by an early freeze. Dependent on weather and the whims of humans for their food, they can lose their nectar sources not only due to drought but also due to mowing or herbicides or just poor planning on the gardener's part. I've seen such damage before.

Out on a walk last spring, wandering down a South Texas road at sunset, I came across a pair of disembodied wings. Just minutes before, I imagined, they had caught the wind and borne some fragile butterfly across the trees. The queen's body strangely absent, all that remained now were the wings, orange and black against the asphalt, orange and black and delicate as ash.

Everywhere they go, it seems, butterflies are somebody's food. Flying, they are caught in the webs of orb-weaving spiders or captured by birds on the wing. Roosting, they are taken by ants and raccoons, possums and mice. Feeding, they are everyone's game—lizards and snakes, beetles and assassin bugs, stink bugs, dragonflies, birds. And, of course, spiders of various kinds.

What I was watching, I finally realized, was a crab spider doing its work. With bodies shorter and broader than those of their kin, the crab spiders, members of the family *Thomisidae*, rely on agility and stealth instead of webs to catch their prey. Living on plants, many lie in wait inside the blooms themselves, trapping insects as they feed.

For one member of the *Misumena* genus in particular, *Misumena vatia,* the task is made easier by a special trick. Initially white, this crab spider has a gift for changing color. As the season progresses and more yellow flowers start to bloom, this spider turns yellow as well. Could it be I was seeing one now? The creature before me was white, all right, but with myriad species to choose from, I was hesitant to say.

What I did know, however, was the way that the spider feeds. Grasping the victim with its clawlike chelicerae, it immediately floods the wound with poison. This venom, which flows from a duct in the creature's claws, has a double role to play. First, and most obviously, it renders the captive harmless. But equally important to the spider, the venom liquifies the prey. All the talk of fangs and jaws notwithstanding, a spider can't really bite a thing. With a mouth fit only for liquid food, it pumps its victim with digestive juices, then drains the insect dry. It eats its kill from the inside out, leaving an empty shell.

Glancing down at the clump of horsemint at my knees, taking in for a moment this small tableau in the leaves, I began to wonder how many more such struggles were going on nearby. Just a few feet away and not long ago, I had come across two broods of caterpillars—one orange-red, the other black—devouring two sunflower plants on the path. Both broods, I suspected, were larvae of the fairly common bordered patch, and both were gone in a matter of days.

But gone where?

The Sound of Water

AFTER THE PANIC, after the swirling and spinning comes the hanging on. Hands pressed against a rough log, you jerk your head back, kick your feet, and feel the air against your anxious face.

I made it, you tell yourself, sure that this will be just like those times you fought for daylight in the deep end of the pool. Clinging to the ridged bark of a pecan with the tips of your fingers, you cough and cough, spewing river water from your startled lungs. You have made it, you think. And then the current pulls you down.

Has water ever been so deep, so blue, so charged with light? More baffled than afraid, you wonder at your own surprise, at your capacity to think in such a state. For an instant, you are not convinced that this is happening to you. It is someone else's body, someone else's dream, someone else's death. And then it hits.

So, you tell yourself without alarm, *this is what it's like to drown.*

Stunned that everything could come to such a sudden end—no warning, no premonitions, no time to be afraid—you think of your daughter, of what she will do when she hears. And then it stops. Your reverie is broken by a gasp. Pushed to the surface, you take a breath, cough, and fling your body hard against the toppled tree. It is all you can do, but it is not enough.

Suddenly, and against all instinct, you know you have to let go. And so you do.

Sinking one last time, you feel yourself propelled beneath the tree and spun out on the other side. Carried by the current and the life jacket riding high against your neck, you let yourself be borne away. Then, passing under a grapevine, you lunge, grab it with both hands, and cling. You are alive.

Coughing and coughing, you finally take a breath. For the first time since your fiberglass canoe was swept into the rock, since you felt the current flip your boat and send you headlong toward the fallen tree, you see your friends. One has somehow reached the bank behind you. The other, arms draped across the trunk of the pecan, has yet to wash downstream.

Together, you and your friend on the bank begin to shout her name. At last, she answers. She is fine, she says. All three of you survived.

Knowing that you can't stay where you are for long, you let go of the vine, bobbing as the current catches you and drives you toward more rocks. Bumping from one to another, you somehow come to rest against the stern of the canoe. You grab for the gunwale and hang on. Remembering to keep the swamped boat downstream, you let it drag you toward a sandbar. There, collapsed on a boulder, you look at your hands again and again, surprised that you are still in your body, surprised that you are alive.

Later, when you are safe and dry and able to ask, you will learn what it was you confronted. "At Old Mill Rapids, there's a real sharp turn to the right," Mike Spencer, the owner of a local canoe livery, will tell you. "There's a tree coming out of the bank on the left, and most of the water goes under that tree. All of the water is pushing you over toward the bank. It could push you and pin you there against the bank."

Although the river is six feet deep beneath that tree, it's not the depth that concerns him. "The water's moving pretty fast right there," this veteran canoeist will explain. "If you've got a canoe in a five-mile-an-hour current and you swamp the boat with the open end upstream, you'd have about two thousand pounds of force between the canoe and whatever stopped it."

Ordinarily, a boater who ends up in the water will want to go downstream feet first. "That's the wrong way to go into a log jam," Spencer will tell you. "This is a last resort, of course, because you don't want to get into this situation, but you need to roll over on your stomach, go head first down the river, and look for a big log to hang onto. Crawl on top of it like you're pulling yourself out of a swimming pool that doesn't have a ladder. With your legs behind you, you can scissor-kick onto the top."

What happens if you're swept beneath the jam? "You may or may not come out the other end," Spencer will admit. "There's all kinds of things under a jam, like limbs. The chances of coming out on the other side are no better than fifty percent. And the longer the jam is, the worse the odds."

"If it's a single log," he will add, "you can get under it and back up with no problem. If you're lucky."

And lucky is how you will feel.

Prepared as you were, and tame as the river can be, you will know that you could have died. "The San Marcos River is a relatively mild river," Mike Spencer will tell you. "People need to give the river respect without being afraid of it. You just need to recognize the hazards and keep yourself out of them." Private dams, rapids, the remnants of early twentieth-century mills—each can be a danger, he will say, but none of them has to be.

For nights thereafter, you will notice as you drift toward sleep, you will hear the sound of water, will feel it pull you down and down into the crystal blue. The sky will slip away, your feet will sink, and you will gasp, then catch yourself in time before you drown.

Not surprisingly, the words from a poem that you read the day before you entered the river will form an eddy in your mind. "Doesn't everything die at last, and too soon?" Mary Oliver asks in "The Summer Day." "Tell me, what is it you plan to do / with your one wild and precious life?"

Your answer, when it comes, will rise up from the depths of sleep, wordless like some primal urge, like hunger or fear, like the sound of water rushing over rocks.

Simple Pleasures

IT WAS THE BEST stand of greenthread that I'd had in years. And with the horsemint, gaillardia, Mexican hat, and winecups blooming too, the display was a pleasure to behold.

Most mornings, those flowers formed a backdrop for the birds I followed from my study window. Most evenings, they were rich with butterflies and bees.

Simple pleasures, they helped me simplify my life. Walking among them, collecting seed as it began to form, I felt the stresses of the day ease up. I felt, for a moment at least, that I was in a place where everything made sense, where nature's economy worked just right.

That's a lot of weight for a small garden to bear, but it's what our gardens do. The swath of flowers by the split-rail fence, the bed by a neighbor's mailbox, the row of herbs along another's drive—whatever their size, our gardens teach us certain things, not the least of which is who and what we are.

Left to themselves, I knew, these flowers along my fence would feed a host of creatures through the early summer months. Left to themselves, they ultimately would go to seed, would sow themselves in the undisturbed earth, would sprout in the early spring rain. To know these things is to know much more than scientific fact. It is, in essence, to know that we can trust the earth, that we can trust our very lives.

Too great a claim perhaps? I don't believe it is. In learning to pay attention to a little patch of ground, we learn to pay attention to the

world. We learn about limits and loss, about nurture and the sub-
tleties of growth, about the power of life itself.

As I write these words, however, what I see from my study window
is a bare place where these flowers grew. Cut down by a county
mowing crew this afternoon, they lie as mulch along the front edge of
our lawn.

Anger, outrage, disbelief—I'll admit that I've felt them all.

When I called my precinct office, I was told that the grass is cut
along the county roads for safety's sake. Visibility for drivers, I
learned, is the sole concern. Fair enough, I said, but I live in a neighborhood, not on a busy county road. Visibility is not an issue when it
comes to my front yard, or my neighbor's, or that of the person down
the street.

No, the real reason that a mowing crew came through my neighborhood today, shredding every wildflower growing along our street
is simply this: the calendar said it was time. Forget all the rain we've
had in recent weeks. Forget that the flowers were still in bloom. Forget
that now they will never go to seed or sprout again next year.

In short, forget to pay attention to the world, and what you end up
with is a machine, cutting a swath through what is beautiful, alive, and
green.

The Infinite Set

FIFTEEN HUNDRED MILES from here, on the side of a mountain in Colorado, a yellow-bellied marmot runs across a hiking trail, stops at the base of a large rock, and begins digging for food in the loose dirt. Sitting nearby in the grass, a woman draws her knees up under her chin and watches in silence.

In her mind, this meadow, this quadrant on the Forest Service map, has suddenly become the universe. For an instant or two, there is nothing in her life but the marmot, the grass, the trail that stretches out ahead of her and disappears into a grove of aspen.

Closing her eyes, the woman imagines a different scene. She is in the mind of the marmot, and what she sees is herself, only farther away and smaller. She is somewhere on the periphery of things, superfluous in the world of the marmot.

When she leaves this meadow forty-five minutes from now, the marmot will imagine that she has ceased to be. He will not wonder where she is going or if she is happy or if she has any life apart from him. Instead, he will continue digging in this patch of dirt, and when it begins to rain later in the day, he will hide underground and imagine that he is alone in the universe.

In a small town in Texas, the woman sits in her study, listening to a thunderstorm rolling in from the west and struggling to remember a cool meadow far away on the side of a mountain. Tonight her universe is a room lined with brown bookshelves, a cursor blinking at her from a computer screen, a dog scratching halfheartedly on a closed door.

Fifteen hundred miles away, darkness is settling across the western slope of the Rockies, and as it falls, a yellow-bellied marmot whistles to his mate across a field of boulders. By thinking of the marmot, the woman can almost see what he sees, hear what he hears. Imagining herself in his place, she can almost feel the wind ruffling the fur on the back of his thick neck.

The marmot cannot imagine her.

Because she is a human being and not a creature living on the side of a mountain, the woman knows certain things. Without having to see him, she knows that she is linked inextricably to the marmot, and to a million other small lives across the planet. And without having to leave this room, she knows that her world intersects not only his but another and another. The infinite set.

Roughly eighty miles north of Corpus Christi, Texas, a man is fishing in Lavaca Bay. What he doesn't realize is that for more than twenty years, the local Alcoa plant discharged large quantities of mercury into this section of the bay. He knows nothing of the benzene and the toluene, the chloroform and the PCBs that have been found in the bay's sediment as well as in the shallow groundwater not far from the shore. And he is unaware that Calhoun County, where Alcoa operates along with Formosa Plastics and other industries, was designated in the late 1980s as one of the ten most polluted counties in the nation.

In short, what he doesn't realize is that any fish he catches in this area of the bay—black drum, speckled seatrout, redfish—will likely be contaminated with mercury. First link between Something and Nothing.

In May of 2003, the woman reads, two lowland gorillas were recovered from the pet trade in Nigeria and returned to their native Cameroon. Captured in 1995 as infants, the endangered animals—named Brighter and Twiggy—were released to live with other primates in the world-famous Limbe Wildlife Centre.

To the poachers who had captured the baby gorillas, and killed their mothers to sell as bushmeat, they were commodities worth as much as $250,000 each. To their owner, they were a symbol of status and wealth. To the Nigerian government, they were a rare success story.

And what are they to themselves? Like the marmot and the woman sitting in her study, each is the center of a small universe.

Sitting in her study, with its brown bookshelves and its forest green walls, the woman imagines herself in the mind of an infant gorilla, stripped from the arms of her dying mother. First link between Something and Nothing.

On the northwest side of San Antonio, members of the Citizens Tree Coalition protest a new development on the frontage road of Interstate 10. While the demonstration is still in progress, crews begin to bulldoze what the local press has referred to as "numerous good-sized trees," including one with a trunk measuring three feet across.

A McDonald's and a Chevron station will be built to take their place.

Listening to the storm outside her window, the woman closes her eyes and thinks of places she has never been, of oceans and deserts and mountains without trails. Tilt the globe just so, she realizes, and each becomes the center of the world, the most important place on earth. Look at the universe just right, and nothing is expendable.

On the side of a mountain in Colorado, a marmot falls asleep and dreams he is alone. Fifteen hundred miles away, in a room lined with books, a woman hears him breathing.

Dark Skies

I'VE MISSED THIS," my daughter said as we stood at the end of the driveway, our eyes turned up to see the stars. "We don't have this kind of sky in town."

As she spoke, I recalled the night, some years before, when she lay for hours, stretched out on the trunk of her car, watching for shooting stars. Now more or less on her own and living in the city, she can seldom see such sights. Now her nighttime sky is filled with the glare of a thousand streetlights and porch lights and the glow of buildings a mile or more away.

Someone, some thing has robbed her of the night.

What does it matter if we can no longer see the stars? "It's just like seeing trees and grass," Dr. Tim Hunter told me when we spoke on the phone not long ago. "You don't need this, but it sure makes the quality of life better."

One of the founders of the International Dark-Sky Association, Hunter is a radiologist at the University of Arizona Medical Center and an amateur astronomer living in Tucson. Like him, about half of the association's more than ten thousand members are hobbyists or part-timers in the field, while another fourth are professionals working in observatories or departments of astronomy. The rest of the membership, which includes people in all fifty states and seventy foreign countries, are "just interested in looking at the pretty night sky."

Founded in 1987, the International Dark-Sky Association was in great part the brainchild of Dr. David Crawford, an emeritus astronomer at Kitt Peak National Observatory, fifty-five miles southwest of Tucson. As long ago as the early 1970s, Crawford and his colleagues had recognized the impact that light pollution was having on their research, and as a result, Crawford went to work learning all he could about effective lighting design.

Today, Hunter said, Crawford serves as volunteer executive director of IDA and spends much of his time writing and speaking on behalf of the organization. What is the gist of the message that he spreads? Quite simply, that outdoor lighting need not be bad lighting.

Without disputing the fact that proper nighttime lighting does contribute to the safety of pedestrians and motorists, IDA contends that light pollution is wasteful and costly, that it impedes the work of astronomers, and that it robs all of us of the "human experience of the inspiring beauty of the cosmos." Moreover, IDA argues, the glare produced by inefficient lighting actually makes such lighting a hazard rather than a help.

The alternatives? When it comes to outdoor lighting, IDA first advocates using the most efficient sources available, such as a low pressure sodium or metal halide lamp. While the inexpensive dusk-to-dawn 175-watt mercury vapor fixture may seem the best choice, it is in reality the most inefficient. That is, its bright light tends to "splatter," creating areas of blinding glare and deep shadows where intruders can hide.

In addition, IDA advises that outdoor fixtures be positioned so that their light shines down rather than up or out, and that a timer or some other form of control be used to avoid waste.

"I think we've been moderately effective," Hunter said of the organization's efforts. "I've seen an enormous change in the amount of public attention to this issue." As of 1989, for example, more than fifty outdoor lighting control ordinances had been enacted throughout Arizona and in key cities in California and Hawaii. Interest in the problem was also growing in far West Texas and in Maine, Wisconsin, and Massachusetts. In 2003, half a dozen states have ordinances against light pollution, and many more have legislation pending.

Given the fact that light pollution costs Americans more than one billion dollars a year in wasted energy, the aims of the International Dark-Sky Association do make a great deal of sense. But economics, I will admit, is far from my main concern.

"Have you ever seen so many stars?" I remember asking my husband several summers ago as we stood beneath the Milky Way in a town in southern Utah. Astounded by the view, I was suddenly made aware—again—of what it is that lures us west year after year.

It's the emptiness, of course, an emptiness filled with rocks and rifts and stars.

"The stars are more than we bargained for," physicist Chet Raymo observes in *Honey from Stone*. "They are thermonuclear furnaces, incandescent with the heat of vanished matter, globes a million miles in diameter, or ten million, or a hundred million, voluptuous presences."

Voluptuous presences. How do I begin to explain why the glow of the outlet mall and the interstate highway and the cement plant down the road disturb me? How do I tell my neighbors that I have no use for streetlights? How do I convince them that I *need* the night?

Standing on my driveway, binoculars in hand, I look to the stars in much the same way that old-time navigators did. Dizzy with distance and speed and the knowledge that I'm not alone, I fix my eyes on a faraway cluster of lights and consider my place on the earth. Celestial navigation, it was once called, the art of looking to the stars to find out where you are.

Minus a chronometer and sextant, not to mention the skill to use them, I am nonetheless conscious of the relative size of things, of the precariousness of planets and stars, of the fragility of earth. Under the clear night sky, with the universe unfolding at my feet, I am strangely certain of my limits, certain of my place. Perhaps something other than the sky could tell me this, but nothing else could plunge me quite so deep into the void, then urge me out again, glad for the presence of light.

A Cry in the Night

FOR THE THIRD NIGHT in a row, I would be staying in the guest house alone—alone, that is, except for the creatures that made this place their home.

"So, have you heard the raccoons?" a friend had asked at lunch earlier in the day. As I listened with amusement, she told me how, on more than a few occasions, she'd been awakened by the resident raccoons and squirrels, how during the night they skittered through the attic of the tile-roofed guest house where she'd stayed any number of times.

"It sounds like they're going to come through the ceiling," she added, her expression telling me that this was more than a figure of speech.

Located just five minutes from downtown, in the section of San Antonio known as Alamo Heights, the Bishop Jones Center takes in roughly twenty acres along a creek that, during heavy rains, still flows into the San Antonio River. The main building on the property contains the offices of the Episcopal Diocese of West Texas. The other building, a large Spanish-style house, serves as a chapel, meeting center, and guest facility for people like me who must stay overnight in the city.

Much of the land itself, also called Cathedral Park, has been left in its natural state or landscaped with native plants, making it ideal habitat for a host of creatures—squirrels, raccoons, opossums, songbirds, and even a few predators.

Late at night, with the lights off and everybody gone, the place can be more than a little eerie. But it was nearly 11:00 P.M. when I finally pulled in, and I was tired—too tired to think about intruders or spirits or other hazards of the night. After eight hours in a meeting room, and another five touring the city with friends from out of state, I had only one thing on my mind—sleep.

Gathering my things and locking the car behind me, I stood beside it for a moment, just listening to the night. It was then, in that second of hesitation, that I heard the spine-chilling sound.

Wuh-wuh-wuh-wuh-ow! Wuh-wuh-wuh-wuh-ow!

Two nights before, having gone to the kitchen for a drink, I had noticed something very like a dog's bark coming from just outside the window. Now the sound was even louder, emanating from the copse of trees ahead.

Owl, I thought, feeling suddenly wide awake. But unlike the high-pitched whinny of a screech owl or the mellow hooting of a great horned owl, this call was like that of an animal in pain or fear or some other state of agitation. Intrigued, I walked directly toward the sound, stopping every few feet to listen.

Almost imperceptibly, I realized, the sound was moving along the roofline of the building to my right. I couldn't see anything at first, but then I caught it, a shape that was undoubtedly the silhouette of an owl.

I was elated. More than that, I was proud to have gotten so close to such a large and usually reclusive bird without scaring it away.

It was only then, when I turned my eyes slightly to the left, that I spotted a dark and brooding figure on the lawn. In the shadow of the trees some twenty feet away, it looked at first to be a hawk or, as it suddenly began to sway and grow in size, a mammal of some kind.

Mesmerized, I watched the creature's back for a second, watched it as it bent and jerked, as it lifted its head and fluffed its silent wings.

Owl, I thought again, afraid to say the word aloud.

I knew that I had been seen.

Turning first its head and then its body, the creature pinned me with a stare before extending its wings, which have a span of nearly four feet, and taking flight—directly toward me. I covered my head and ran.

"I've seen it too," a woman familiar with Cathedral Park told me some days later. "It's as big as a three-year-old child."

And so it seemed.

Hoping to learn more about the creature I had seen, I called a wildlife biologist with the Austin Nature and Science Center. "That's not their typical response," he explained when I told him of my experience. Rather than flying toward me, he said, an owl would normally just snap its beak loudly, fluff up, and adopt a posture of defense. But with a building at its back—who knows, he admitted. The scenario could change.

He had seen it happen more than once.

When I asked him if he had ever had a threatening encounter with an owl himself, the biologist said he had. "I've been 'footed' before," he said, "footed, but never really hurt."

And so, I inquired at last, what, exactly, had I seen? Not a great horned owl, judging from its call and lack of "ear" tufts. And not a barn owl either, given that the bird I saw was dark. Quite probably, I learned, it was a barred owl, a stocky gray-brown owl with a large, round head and dark brown eyes. Though best known for its call of *who cooks for you? who cooks for you all?* it has a repertoire that includes a variety of barks and clucks as well.

Precisely the calls I had heard.

Most likely members of the subspecies *Strix varia helveola*, which occurs only in south-central Texas, these owls were no doubt a breeding pair; the low-pitched bark I noted was the territorial call of the male. Mated for life, these two could be expected to live for a decade or more, all in the general vicinity of Cathedral Park.

Science has its name for the barred owl, and so do those who favor more descriptive terms, such as "swamp owl," "rain owl," "round-headed owl." But the name I prefer is Mystery, that which listens for us in the dark. Don't be surprised, this bird reminds me, if Mystery hears you, if it springs up feather soft and fierce out of the shadows, its cry familiar, yet like nothing that you've ever heard before.

Cicada

MY FRIEND had just returned from Ireland, and there on the table between us sat the little box she had brought me filled with treasures—a snippet of bell heather from the Iveraugh Peninsula, a small green rock from St. Finan's Bay, a piece of mica from St. Kevin's cell at Glendalough. No bones of the saints, no pieces of the true cross, but holy relics just the same.

"I've brought you something, too," I told her, reaching into my open purse and pulling out an object I had wrapped in a single Kleenex. Removing the paper, I carefully placed the gift in front of my friend. She responded with a high, thin laugh.

"A cicada!" she squealed, setting the insect husk on her outstretched palm. "Oh my."

Like my cat, which deposits the bodies of dead and dying birds and mice on my doorstep as a boon, I had brought my friend a trophy, a memento of my latest trip. Unlike my cat, however, I had chosen to do so in a very public place—more specifically, in an upscale restaurant filled with society matrons finishing their lunch.

I'm perverse that way, I guess.

As I told my friend, who continued to study the creature as I talked, I had found the cicada while out on an afternoon walk. Amazed by its perfection, by the lack of damage it had suffered from the rain and sun, I had picked it up, admired it, and slipped it into the pocket of my shorts. It, and another one much like it, had been my only souvenirs from a four-day stay in the South Texas town of Castroville, where I'd gone for an end-of-July retreat.

"I need a real vacation," I had thought two weeks earlier, as my husband and I flew home from a hectic few days in Montana. Having traveled to Missoula for a conference, I had spent most of my time there indoors, talking, listening, brushing elbows with a handful of friends and a host of people whom I'd never met. The experience, quite simply, had worn me out.

"I need some down time," I'd told my friend as soon as I returned. And it was she who'd suggested the historic little town of Castroville, with its Alsatian restaurants, its nineteenth-century buildings, its murky river winding through the trees.

The place where I'd chosen to stay was equally picturesque. Built in the 1870s as the first motherhouse for the Sisters of Divine Providence in the United States, Moye Center is now an eclectic collection of buildings situated on several acres not far from the town's main square. Once a convent, and then for many years a school, it has been a retreat center since 1985.

Arriving on a Monday afternoon, I wasn't long in discovering what there was to do in Castroville. Sleeping—that was good for a start, I realized, and so was sitting on the upstairs porch. With the entire place to myself, and my schedule very much my own, I could read when I wanted, write when I wanted, and come and go as I pleased.

Morning and afternoon walks became highlights of the day.

Ignoring the "Historic Walking Tour" signs, another form of perversity I suspect, I meandered past the old church, through a neighborhood, and down to a park, where debris from the recent floods still hung from the tops of the trees.

A circuitous route, my course took me past a house where pens of gaudy roosters crowed. *Fighting cocks*, I wondered? It took me past fences laced with blooming coral vine, past shoulder-high zinnias and giant sunflowers with heads as big as dinner plates. Littered with green pecans, the sidewalk wound at last through the remnants of a small downtown.

Except for the church, only the little meat market, with its wooden screen doors and its box fan whirring in the window, seemed to be in use. The rest of the square looked dead.

Languid evening, rich with the liquid song of doves, last golden hours of the late summer day—this was the time I cherished most. And it was then, as I strolled along a crooked sidewalk in the shade, that I saw the dead cicada lying in my path.

More often heard than seen, dogday cicadas or harvestflies appear at the height of the summer heat. Unlike periodical cicadas, which infest a different location every thirteen to seventeen years, these creatures emerge at the same sites every year. Taking roughly two years to hatch, mature, and shed their nymphal skins, full-grown cicadas live for just a month. During this time, however, the males fill the summer evenings with their song, a sound that one field guide likens to "a circular saw cutting through a board."

Having sung their song, having mated and laid their eggs, the cicadas soon begin to die, littering lawns and sidewalks with what is left of their brilliant selves. Some will be crushed underfoot or swept away in the rain. Others, the newly dead perhaps, will be picked up by curious children or by adults with their eyes on the ground.

What kind of relic does a dead cicada make? Having brought one home for myself as well as my friend, having set it beside the box with the slip of heather and the green rock and the shiny stone from St. Kevin's Irish cell, I wonder—four months later—exactly what it means.

Holding the creature in my hand, turning it just so in the light, I am caught, again, by its perfection. Wings like plastic wrap stretched over lime green ribs, avocado back inlaid with black and gold, beads of emerald on the underside of its large rear wings—how can such a thing exist?

Weighing nothing, the dead cicada rattles as it slides across my hand. Empty now, its life used up in a few short weeks, this husk is beautiful but mute. Holding the dead cicada on my open palm, I imagine how it felt as it spent itself in a frenzy of lusty song, how it felt as its wings whirred on a summer night, how it felt as it finally fell to earth.

Perfection in Summer

SOMEWHERE ABOVE the moonlit driveway, an invisible line of geese is heading south for the winter. It is too early for this, I tell myself, too early for the season to be changing again. Perhaps the sound I hear is only tree frogs croaking in the brush next door, or children several houses away. I am not easily convinced.

"Look, they even have a light," my husband says, laughing as he points to a cluster of red and yellow dots in the sky. It is an airplane, of course, only a little brighter than the field of stars around it. But in our imagination, the cluster of lights is leading the flock south.

One minute, two, five minutes pass, and the chorus has faded to a single bird's call. Had we come outside any later, we would have missed the show altogether.

Fall is like that here in Central Texas. Except for the occasional blue norther that sweeps across the hills in late October, there are seldom any clear-cut signs of the seasons. One day it's summer, and the next it's fall—and all because someone has decreed it so.

Only a week ago, it would have been daylight still. There would have been children on bicycles riding past our house, people in their yards, watering the grass or bringing in the mail. It is, after all, just a quarter past seven, and far too early for dark.

"Have you adjusted to the time change?" a friend asked me this afternoon. I told her that I had, but that is only half true. I let go of things, even daylight, reluctantly.

I am surprised to find myself hanging on to summer this way. Of all the seasons, it is the one I enjoy least. Too hot, too dry, too bug-infested to suit me—in most cases, the summer can't pass soon enough.

But is it really summer that I cling to so tenaciously? No, it is only the memory of summer.

In the back of my mind somewhere, buried beneath the mental artifacts of several decades, is an ideal summer. Filled with cousins and homemade peppermint ice cream, green metal lawn chairs arranged in semicircles under pecan trees, the hum of my aunt's window air conditioner, children with jars of fireflies playing on my uncle's lawn—in my memory, there is only one summer, and it is per-fection.

But arbitrarily now, the clock and the calendar tell me that this season is over. Without warning, without a sign, they have pushed me into autumn.

There is a single red leaf on the tallow tree in my front yard. It has hung there for weeks, refusing to drop. In the back yard, our big yellow Lab has spent the day curled up in the shade. To him, there is no logic in the seasons, no artificial distinction between one and the next. Instead, there are only heat and cold, sun and shade.

Like him, I take comfort in familiar things, in the way the lawn feels cool on my feet just after mowing, in the long, leafy shadow the Spanish oak makes across the front yard.

No, it is not summer that I mourn. It is something else, something just as warm and familiar.

"Most of us resist change," a friend said the other day. A change of season, a change of scene—we say we welcome these things, but when the time comes to move forward, we hold on to what we know, and even what we hate.

One day I was the mother of a helpless child just learning to pull up on the coffee table. Another day, without warning, I discover this child preening in the bathroom mirror, looking more beautiful than I can believe. I am letting go of her reluctantly.

One day, too, I was a father's daughter, lowest branch on the family tree. But another day, with far too little warning, I found myself at the top. I am adjusting reluctantly.

Do most of us resist change? I suspect we do, especially when the lines between one season and the next are blurred. Where does the child end and the man or woman begin? What separates youth and middle age? Middle age and "maturity"? I do not feel particularly older or wiser or better equipped, but in the last few years I have felt myself being nudged toward invisible lines of one sort or another. I cross them reluctantly.

In a matter of weeks, if not days, the weather will be changing. One November afternoon, a line of blue clouds will roll across the hills from the north, bringing down the first real chill of autumn.

Finally convinced that summer is over, I will light a fire in the fireplace, pour a glass of wine, and listen for geese flying south by moonlight.

Where Goodness Goes

Pushing away the mulch that had covered the bed since early spring, I was surprised to find that the soil had faded to a dusty gray. Weeks since the last good rain, the ground had grown brittle and dry. Even the air, which was usually thick and humid, had been wrung to a final thinness.

Summer was wearing down.

I suppose I should have been disappointed somehow, saddened by the fact that the months of work I had put into this garden would soon be lost to winter. But strangely enough, I was not. If anything, I was relieved to step back, to watch this final burst of color, to wait patiently for frost. It was the end of something, all right, but also the beginning.

Just above the tired zinnias, a single zebra longwing floated on the warm October air. More nervous in their flight, three anonymous orange butterflies took turns landing nearby, probing the yellow center of each flower with their long tongues. Beside the bottom rung of the fence, a lone bee flitted between the blossoms of the sunflower golden-eye.

It was hard to imagine that in another month, perhaps less, all this would fade to dull brown. "Nothing gold can stay," Frost wrote. "Leaf subsides to leaf."

It is the lesson that every gardener knows.

When we moved onto this place almost twenty-five years ago, I had no idea how it would look in the future, and I certainly had no plan. Content to dream from one season to the next, to experiment casually with this or that, I came to where I am quite haphazardly, quite by chance.

From the fullness of summer to the waning of fall, the gardener thinks in terms of an ongoing cycle of replenishment and loss. The larkspur seeds go into the soil in October, they come up in the rain of December, grow through the winter, and bloom in April or May. Dying, they return themselves to the earth, where they are nurtured for another season.

Not surprisingly, we westerners are often criticized for our tendency to think in long, straight lines, to imagine that where we are going is nothing at all like where we have been. Movement is progress, we believe, and progress is everything.

"The cyclic vision, on the other hand, sees our life ultimately not as a cross-country journey or a voyage of discovery, but as a circular dance in which certain basic and necessary patterns are repeated endlessly," Wendell Berry writes in "Discipline and Hope."

I was walking through the woods in the late afternoon, searching for one of the cats, when my eye was caught by something lying in the grass. At first it appeared to be nothing more than a pile of light-colored fur, the sort of pile that might be left after I've given the dog a trim. But bending down for a closer look, I realized that it was the remains of an animal.

What I had found, I quickly discovered, was the skeleton of a small opossum. With its pointed snout and menacing teeth, it was the skull that gave this away.

Picking it up and brushing off the leaves, I began to wonder what drove this creature out of its home in the garage, or under the shed, and into the woods to die. Was it illness, or simple age? Was it an injury, or wounds from a fatal fight? And why, I was curious to know, were the other animals content to let it lie here so long, apparently undisturbed?

I suspected that I would find no answer to my questions, so I contented myself with the thought that this place, this little patch of soil in the woods, would be richer for the possum's loss. Indeed, in this simple equation of life and death, nothing can be lost for good.

"All of us are in motion, rising out of previous forms and advancing into new ones, and beauty is the best name I know for the ways in which our shape-shifting nature pursues its changes," John Daniel writes in "Some Mortal Speculations."

It is easy enough to accept the alchemy of the garden—the cosmos that wither and die, the ironweed that gives up its seeds to the soil, the artemesia that freezes back, only to return from the roots in spring. It is easy to understand that the stems and leaves of summer will in time become the earth itself.

What is far more difficult, and more painful, is to find solace in the deaths of those we love.

It was dusk when I returned to the garden, and the butterflies that an hour ago had been shimmering in the sun were gone. They would no doubt be back tomorrow, but from the chill in the air, I realized that they would soon disappear for good.

What of those people whose lives have somehow brushed against ours? What of the mothers and fathers, the teachers and friends whose stories have merged with our own? Are we to think that they have simply ceased to be?

Or are we, watching the sun set at the end of an autumn day, to realize that they are somehow part of us?

Where does goodness go when the body dies? And what of the dreams and the little kindnesses that nurture our common life? Like last year's oak leaves, turned and turned into the soil, they feed us still.

Nothing, as the gardener knows, is ever lost.

Why Write about Nature

For Pablo
September 8, 1994–October 18, 1994

L ILAC AND GOLD, the flowers of autumn rise resplendent
from the brittle grass. Gayfeather and goldenrod, frostweed
and sunflower goldeneye—they shine against the backdrop of
a gray, soft-focus sky.

It is just after first light on this stretch of Texas highway, and the
spray from the whooshing tires sings against the bottom of the car.
Rising from bed at six on a Saturday morning, I had grumbled about
getting such an early start. But here on the empty road now I'm content, glad for the taste of solitude.

This drive toward the coast is one I've made at least a hundred
times. And because I once saw a patch of Michaelmas daisies in
bloom beside the porch of a weathered house, I find myself glancing
in that direction each time I pass. Today, though, the yard is empty,
save for a rusty pickup parked beneath the branches of an ample oak.

What can be said for such a landscape? What can be made of the
simple fact that where liatris blooms this fall, huisache will blossom in
the spring?

"Change is a measure of time and, in the autumn, time seems
speeded up," Edwin Way Teale writes in *October.* "What was, is not,
and never again will be; what is, is change."

"Why write about nature?" a friend asked me not long ago. Why say what seems so obvious to the eye? It is not for lack of imagination that she finds this habit odd, or for lack of appreciation of the earth. It is the weight of words that puts her off, I suspect, the burden of language on what should be known by sense alone.

Why write about nature? The question recurs as I drive through the fog of an autumn morning. Is it not enough to see the harrier, the marsh hawk, perched atop the telephone pole, to feel the touch of velvet-leaf mallow against my skin, to smell the dampness of the pungent earth? Must I write of these things as well?

I must.

"It makes them more real," I told my friend, ineptly, when she asked. That is part of the answer, but only part.

Physical being that I am, I know the world primarily as it comes to me through my fingertips. I know it through the polished surface of a snail's shell, the nubby cap of an acorn, the density of wet clay. Piece by piece, I collect the parts, assembling it as I go.

But what of that hidden life, that life that exists beyond my grasp? It is no less real, I suspect, and yet when I try to give it form or weight or color it disappears, ethereal as sunlight. Holding just the memory of its brilliance, I am rendered mute and blind, senseless in the face of a mystery I can't speak.

Shall I call it Transience? Mutability? Loss? If so, what is its shape? How will I know it when it looks me in the eye?

Creature of sinew and soul, I feel my life go deeper underground, potato-like, spreading out beneath me in a web of roots. Sightless, I can only sense what this other self must know.

Along an empty highway, an hour south of my home, a stand of Maximilian sunflowers blazes out against a hedgerow of elm and oak. All the more beautiful for their unexpectedness, they will bloom for a week or two and fade, turning brittle in the first November chill.

How does the intellect perceive impermanence and change? How does it comprehend the fact that a life can flourish for a season, die, and vanish like the morning fog? Fragility, evanescence, the delicacy of beauty brought too swiftly to an end—what the mind rejects, the body surely knows.

Why write about nature? Spirit and flesh, I am nonetheless part of the earth. And earth it is that teaches me the mysteries of love and loss.

How can I understand that what is absent is not gone, that what has ended is not finished, that what is taken is returned as more than memory?

I can't.

What I can do, though, is listen for the sound of the sandhill cranes flying high above my house this fall, feel the supple shoots of next spring's phlox, memorize the curve and hue of Michaelmas daisies in full bloom. What I can do is live as though beauty matters, as if its imprint on the soul never fades.

Lost Maples

SITTING ON the limestone lip of a spring-fed pool, soothed by the sound of water as it trickles lightly over rock, I imagine I am alone. I imagine I am here with only these gray stones, with these clumps of maidenhair fern, with this single wounded butterfly—a red admiral with a clipped and tattered wing—struggling to free itself from the surface tension of the pool.

I imagine I am insulated by this deep blue dome of sky. And I imagine that the red of the Texas oaks is a kind of energy, that I am charged by their color, by their roughness, by their size.

I am imagining all of this and more when a voice rumbles toward me from the trail above.

"There're people down there," one of the hikers tells the others in his group. Feeling as if I'm suddenly on display, part of the local fauna perhaps, I close my journal and scoot into the gritty shadows of the wall behind my back.

Another group of hikers, louder than the first and carrying a pair of screaming toddlers, follows quickly on their heels. Next comes a troop of Boy Scouts, running ahead of their leader and skidding on the gravel path. It is enough. The illusion of solitude broken, I stuff my journal and camera into my pack, hoist the rucksack onto my back, and clamber from my refuge in the rocks.

To be sure, autumn is the busiest of seasons here at Lost Maples State Natural Area, and even though the park staff say the trees are less spectacular than usual this year, the place is overrun with guests. "Park visitation numbers in the thousands on the weekends of the maximum color change," one of my guidebooks tells me, "and campers must have reservations."

Reservations—fortunately, I'd seen to those two months ago. And fortunately, my husband and I and a group of students from my honors nature writing class had arrived ahead of the crush. More precisely, we'd arrived after dark the night before. Stopping our university van in a parking area near the trailhead to the primitive camping sites, we had unloaded our gear, found our flashlights, and begun our mile-long hike beneath a clear but moonless sky.

Crossing Can Creek several times, careful to place our boots just so on the rocks that formed our makeshift bridge, we came to a halt at last beside a narrow chain of ponds. Here and there, other campers were finishing their evening chores; here and there, a lantern glowed, illuminating the gnarly limbs of the Texas oaks.

Eventually we settled on a spot across the trail from the ponds and, after finding semilevel places for our tents, quickly raised them in the dark.

"This can be the kitchen," one of the students announced when we were through, smiling as he gestured toward a ring of jagged rocks. Following his lead, we set our Coleman stove nearby, put a pot of water on to boil, and sat around the lantern, shivering with cold.

"You'd think it was putting out heat," another student quipped when he noticed the way we were huddling around our battery-powered lamp.

"The illusion of warmth," I remarked. "Whatever works."

Soon, though, we were sipping real hot tea from our insulated mugs; we were studying the night sky, brimful of stars, and letting go of all that kept us weighted to the earth.

"There's Orion," someone noted, pointing to the stars that formed the hunter's belt. Squinting, I tried to imagine the shape that had given the constellation its name. As always, though, I failed. As always, I would simply have to trust that it was there.

Not satisfied with the view from our campsite, the students elected to hike to the top of the hill. Less adventurous, and growing colder by the minute, my husband and I chose instead the relative warmth of our tent.

I was not quite asleep when the noise began, roughly an hour and a half later. It wasn't the students, I realized, because I'd heard them return some time before. What it was, though, was anybody's guess. A parade of children, squealing, laughing, pulling an ox-cart full of rocks? I would've wagered that it was.

Just after dawn the following morning, we discovered that during the night a troop of Boy Scouts had set up camp right down the trail beside the pond. Already, while we were still stumbling from our tents, they were hard at work—running, screaming, pushing one another through the loose rocks on the hill.

So much for our peace and quiet, I thought as I watched the three campers across from us pack up their things and leave. They knew how to time it right.

We were still sitting around the stove, finishing our pancakes and coffee, when two teenagers appeared at the site the trio of men had just left. Piling their gear on the ground, they immediately started looking for a place to erect their tent.

"What's he doing?" I asked one of the students as we watched from across the way. Silver hatchet in his hand, the young man appeared to be hacking away at the trunk of a large oak. Chopping a little here, chopping a little there, he chopped with no apparent goal. He was chopping, it seemed, simply because he could.

I would think of this young man later in the day as I walked down the Maple Trail, admiring the autumn colors of the leaves. And I would think of him also when I stopped beside the dry riverbed to watch two children clambering across the rocks, ignoring the "keep off" signs and firing cap guns as they ran. I would think of him, too, when forced off the trail by a group of people walking three abreast, when jostled by the brother and sister running from their parents, when surprised by the toddler on his Big Wheel coming down the path.

"Why come here to do that?" I overheard a woman say as she listened to the sound of cap guns ringing through the autumn air.

Why indeed? I wondered, puzzled by the people rushing by, puzzled by their haste, their noise, their lack of interest in this wild and primal place.

Why come here, I wondered, if earth and trees and stars are not enough?

The Scent of Sycamore

THIS IS WHAT YOU DO, I think as I kneel beside my mother's driveway, pulling spikes of grass from her bed of moss rose and heather. This is what you do when there is nothing to be done.

For a week now, I have watched as my mother has grown smaller and more frail. For a week now, I have watched as layer upon layer of her public self has dropped away, leaving a hard kernel of memory and love.

"They think it's cancer," my sister had said when she called just two weeks before. "It doesn't look good."

And it wasn't.

Seven years after our father's death from the same disease, we are back on the cancer ward, back on the floor where families gather in twos and threes at the ends of hallways or stand whispering among themselves outside an open door.

It is surprising how quickly we fall back into the rhythm of pain and loss.

"Two weeks ago, I was pulling weeds in the garden," my mother says, sounding slightly more puzzled than angry. Today it is all she can do to move from the bed to the chair; tomorrow it will be all she can do to sit up.

That's the way things go sometimes. One day you're cheering at your granddaughter's high school graduation, the next you're wondering about that pain you've had since Easter. No sirens, no bells, just the certain, swift unraveling of all you've ever been.

"I feel just like a baby," my mother says on her second day home from the hospital.

"I know," I tell her, though I can't really know at all.

Forced to return to the hospital the following day, my mother wears the wearied look of one betrayed—betrayed by a body she knows is giving out.

It is Monday when one of the nurses tells us that our mother may not last the week. It is Tuesday evening when she dies. It is as simple and as utterly complex as that.

I have imagined, for some reason I can't understand, that writing about my mother's death would be easy, that the words would simply flow unchecked. Instead, just the opposite has occurred.

To sit with someone during the last two weeks of her life, to watch her weaken and to listen as she breathes her final breath—to do these things, I have discovered, is to be in a place you have never been before. It is real, all right, but like walking in space or landing on the moon, it has no equivalent on earth.

Coming back, you might as well say that you're learned to eat fire or that you know what it is to have lead for bones. The experience is just that strange, and just that impossible to describe.

You are different now, you realize, but not in ways that anyone can see. Rising from your desk to get a cup of coffee, you expect someone to stop you in the hall and say, quite matter-of-factly, "I notice that you have lost a leg," or "Your hair has turned to rivulets of ice." But no one does.

What, then, can be said? Only that you have been to the center of the earth and come back, alive but shaken. Only that you have lost your moorings and been set adrift on a windless sea.

"Humankind cannot bear very much reality," you remind yourself, recalling T. S. Eliot's words. And so you tend to speak in metaphors, in a language that carries the truth inside itself like an embryo. One day you will hold it, but not today.

For now you are doing well to grasp at images, to imagine the notes of a familiar song or to catch the fragrance of vanilla rising from someplace in the back of your mind. Robbed of reason, you become a creature of sense again, running your bare fingers through her sandy flowerbed, breathing the scent of sycamore in the center of her small yard.

"We Americans don't know how to deal with death," her doctor says as we sit around a table at the end of a quiet hall. "We haven't learned to see it as part of the cycle."

Just as we have lost a mother tonight, he has lost a patient and a friend. "I need this as much as you," he says of the nearly two hours we will spend together talking.

It is a way of getting through the night.

In the days that follow, there will be other ways of working through our grief. Standing in my sister's kitchen, we will speak of the nurses who salved our mother's spirit as well as tending to her pain. We will hug our friends and eat their homemade casseroles, we will tell old stories and watch the moon rising brightly over the bay behind the house.

One quiet afternoon, a day or two after her death, I will make a new compost pile in the corner of the lawn.

Before the week is out, each of us—my brother, my sister, and I—will claim a special keepsake to carry home. For one of us it will be the little calendar she kept in an envelope in her drawer, the calendar our father used to mark off the days until their wedding. For another it will be a chipped pie plate or her ragged copy of *Anna Karenina*.

More important, each will carry with us what we found best in her—her quirky sense of humor, her questioning mind, her sense of fairness and loyalty, her love of the earth, her faith.

"It will take time," friends remind us. "You have to give it time."

And so, for now, we let our grief wash over us like salt water on an open wound, welcoming the pain as a sign that healing has begun.

In Search of the Wisdom of the Body

THE THREAT of real winter having passed again for another few days, I have just finished moving roughly twenty potted plants from their spot in front of the fireplace to the deck where they normally sit. And now, with each one back in its proper place, each set just so in the little ring its saucer has left on the wood, I can rock in my deck chair in peace.

Here in mid-December, the late morning heat feels odd. It is odd, too, to catch the sight of migratory birds not due for another month or so—robins flitting through the undergrowth with the sparrows, waxwings whistling overhead. Caught unaware by the arrival of these winter drifters, I am likewise caught unaware by the season, by the preparations for Christmas going on around me. Tied to the academic calendar as I am, I am only now beginning to think of the holiday break at all. Instead, I've been computing final grades, reading student evaluations, and cleaning out cluttered files.

It was only a few days ago, in fact, that I finally got around to removing the Halloween pumpkin from the porch and tossing out the gourds that had sat on the hutch too long. Now, with Christmas just two weeks away, there isn't a gift or a roll of new wrapping paper in the house. I am clearly out of sync.

More to the point, this mishmash of seasons, of weather, of wildlife passing through for the winter—or the week—has left me tired; these raveled edges of the year have left me worn.

"I spent some time Saturday redoing the mantel for Advent," a friend wrote a couple of weeks ago. Reading her description not only of the way it looked but also of the way it felt to decorate this space, I sensed an odd reaction in myself—pure jealousy, I suspect.

With a semester of grading essays almost behind me, and final exams just ahead, I coveted the leisure of a weekend spent attending to my house. What is it that would make me, a person who ordinarily scorns housework and the other domestic arts, actually want to do such a thing?

One explanation, and a fairly obvious one at that, is that my brain is overworked. After fifteen weeks of wondering if a single thing I say is sinking in, I'm ready for a mental respite, some down time for my mind. I'm tired of worrying that my students may not grasp Thoreau, that they may miss the point of the essays they read, may leave my class no more observant or articulate than they were when they began.

But beyond this need imposed by sheer exhaustion, I have sensed a more positive force as well.

"I love this activity, this adorning of the mantel in accord with the liturgical season," my friend had told me.

Like her, I frequently reach the point of saturation, the point where what is academic and abstract quite simply won't soak in. Increasingly, in fact, I find that what I know as true—true about the world, about myself, about the other people in my life—comes less through my mind and more through the soles of my feet, through every nerve, every noise, every light impulse that strikes my eye.

What some have called "the wisdom of the body" is what I seek this time of year. It is the visceral gesture that I crave.

And so it is that as the days go on, I will snip boughs of rosemary for the mantel, will listen for the crackle of oak leaves underfoot, will light candles, run my fingers through the cat's new winter coat, catch the scent of something stirring in the wind.

Lost to what is reasonable, to what appeals to the rational mind, I will be content to spend this season of incarnation as I must. Lost to those things I can explain, I lean back in my deck chair, listen for the wispy flight of waxwings, and wait for my body to speak.

Memories Blooming
Eternally in the Mind

I HAVE FINALLY CUT the sunflowers that bloomed house high in the prime of summer. Growing there along the driveway, towering as they did above the horsemint and the beebalm and the sage, they seemed out of place at times. But in their exuberance, they also seemed a gift, unwatered and unplanned.

Dragging their brittle stalks to the brush pile near the street, I leave a trail of crushed seeds in my wake. Come spring, I imagine, sunflowers will rise through the asphalt like corn, will overtake the lawn, will lift the house from its small foundation. I imagine them lifting me as well, bearing me up on rough leaves toward the sun.

It is the gardener's prerogative to dream.

Turning on the hose, I begin the slow progression from one flowerbed to the next, taking inventory as I walk. It has been a difficult summer, seeming all the worse for the ample spring, and more than a few of the plants I've nursed through other less stressful years have disappeared. The purple salvia, the Russian sage, the passionflower vine, the ox-eye daisies—in the anonymity of leaf litter, one is as formless as the next, one as much a part of the dry earth as the other.

I am tempted to kneel here, to stir the soil with my bare hand and search for some remnant of stem or root. But not wanting to risk disappointment, I move on, aiming a stream of water toward the coral honeysuckle that spills across the fence.

Oblivious to what is happening around me, I hardly notice when our tortoiseshell cat appears at my feet, mewing and brushing back and forth against my ankles with her wispy fur. Minus our big orange tom, which we buried a month ago, she seems almost lost these days, strangely eager for human contact.

It is a feeling I can more than understand.

Five months—that's how long it's been since my mother and I stood here in the glow of a May afternoon, admiring the blooms of the antique roses, the gaillardia, the Drummond's phlox. It might as easily have been a decade, or an hour.

I should write to her about this, I catch myself thinking at least once a day. And then it clicks.

Back in the garden, where there is neither past nor future, all time is gathered into a single moment, eternally present in the mind.

Scene 1: A woman stands on a path of cedar flakes, holding a tortoiseshell cat with one hand and a garden hose with the other. Leaning over, she places the lip of the hose at the base of a *Gerbera* daisy and watches as the water soaks down into the soil. The plants, she remembers as if for the first time, had been her mother's, had been growing in a pot on her mother's patio at the time of her death, had been packed with the family rocker and the box of books and brought to this garden three hours' drive away.

She makes sure to water it well.

Scene 2: Walking through her garden, a woman stops to run her hand across a boulder. White and rough, it was at one time part of a jetty, one stone among many stretching into a narrow bay. Even now, years after she brought it from her parents' home on the Texas coast, she wonders how her father managed to lift it, to drag it from the water and plant it on his lawn.

Resigned to ignorance about such things, she presses her hand against the warm stone and imagines that she hears the sea.

Scene 3: It is 1993. Or 1980. A woman watches while her mother, kneeling on a patch of rocky soil, lowers a small Mexican olive tree into a shallow hole. Ten feet away, a husband and wife sit side by side in a wooden swing, sipping iced tea laced with mint. Purring softly, an orange tomcat curls up between them and falls asleep.

A young girl, who is three or eighteen, depending on the light, stands in the center of the yard, calling her cocker spaniel. In the background, an olive tree blooms, its white flowers iridescent against the Central Texas sky.

It is spring, or the middle of winter. A man in a light gray windbreaker walks toward the house with his granddaughter. He is telling her a story, or saying nothing at all.

In this moment, this frozen image, all moments have converged as one. In this moment, all is present in the mind.

> *. . . Time past and time future*
> *Allow but a little consciousness.*
> *To be conscious is not to be in time*
> *But only in time can the moment in the rose-garden,*
> *The moment in the arbour where the rain beat,*
> *The moment in the draughty church at smokefall*
> *Be remembered; involved with past and future.*
> *Only through time is time conquered.*

Standing on the narrow path, holding a tortoiseshell cat with one hand and a garden hose with the other, I glance toward the empty place where sunflowers once towered above the asphalt drive. In my memory, it is May and they are blooming, eternally blooming in the mind.

I should write to her, I tell myself. And then it clicks.

Grace

Brushed by a
Thousand Wings

FROM MY STUDY WINDOW, they appear as puffs of thistle-down, these waves of autumn butterflies that drift so lithely past our house. Now swirling, now spinning, now spilling out across the lawn, they are coins sparkling in the mid-September sun, silver as light, spending themselves in a frenzy of short-lived flight.

Distracted as I am by the sight of a thousand butterflies, I turn off my stereo, press "Save" on my computer, and head outside for a closer look. Even at this distance, though, it is hard to tell just what it is I see.

Clouded sulphur. Gulf fritillary. Delaware skipper. As easy as it is to say the names, not one of them will fit the creatures flitting past my face. Too fast, too small, too much like bursts of light to pin down with a word, they skirt the labels I would use to own them.

And so, standing at the end of my driveway between the bed of wildflowers and the spiny pyracantha, I let myself be wound up in a mystery, surrounded by the silent fluttering of wings.

"Does sense so stale that it must needs derange / the world to know it?" Richard Wilbur asks in his poem "Praise in Summer." Drawn first to metaphors and then to scientific names, do I, too, struggle so with language that I let experience drift by?

Closing my eyes, I imagine being carried in the wake of a thousand butterflies, being carried farther and farther into the textured world of sense.

"Have you seen them?" my neighbor asks when she calls not twenty minutes later. "Can you tell us what they are?"

I can't, I inform her. But secretly, I wish I could.

Wrestling unsuccessfully against this need to know, this need to fix the beautiful with a taxonomic term, I spend a good part of the next day on the phone.

"Libytheidae," my friend the entomologist says when I describe the sight I've seen. "Snout butterflies."

Standing at the edge of the driveway late that afternoon, I watch again as clouds of butterflies move past me, skimming the tops of the cholla, the bur oak, the clumps of blooming zexmenia. Finally, when a single butterfly lands on the leaf of an antique rose, I reach out and capture it, grasping its closed wings carefully between my thumb and finger.

Except for its fragility, for the paper thinness of its wings; except for its upturned "snout," the two furry receptors on either side of its mouth; except for the orangy brown of its forewings, the mottled gray with hints of pink and lavender below; except for its gift for camouflaging itself as a leaf; except for the total unlikelihood that such a being should exist—except for these things, this creature is unremarkable in every way.

Feeling it begin to struggle in my fingers, I let the butterfly go, following it with my eyes as it loops in air, as it settles on the rock rose, as it drifts across the Turk's cap toward the woods.

Libytheana bachmanii. Libytheana larvata. Snout butterfly. What shall I call this miracle of nature? What shall I call this coming together of substance and dream, this tenuous meeting of air and wing?

Sitting on the limestone step just off my deck, I am inches from a bed of garlic chives abloom in white. I am inches from the red of the *Salvia greggii,* the blue of the indigo spires. I am inches from an entourage of butterflies and hummingbirds and bees.

How odd, I think after such a bone-dry summer. How odd the

way life waits until its time is right, until, at once and in one place, it can play out its extravagance in the bloom of a swath of oxblood lilies or a thousand autumn butterflies in flight. How odd, I think, and how fortuitous for us.

Snout butterflies, I have read, are particularly prolific after periods of extended drought followed by heavy rains. Waiting in the chrysalis stage until the environmental cues are right, they emerge by the thousands, migrating—or "wandering," as writer/photographer Geyata Ajilvsgi tells me—and ultimately laying their eggs on the leaves of their favorite food plant, the hackberry tree.

I know these things, all right, but what is it that I know?

Watching a wave of butterflies on an afternoon in mid-September, I am struck by what I do not understand, by the inability of language to contain the numinous, by the poverty of words. I am struck by what is beautiful, illogical, and strange. I am brushed by a thousand wings.

Knowing Our Place

HAVING WALKED A MILE or so from the main house, the strap of my campstool slung over my shoulder, my journal and another book tucked tightly underneath my arm, I am sitting in the shade of a live oak on the edge of a caliche road. At my feet, a clump of Mexican hat is playing out the last of its summer bloom. Behind it, waxy-leafed snow-on-the-mountain bends limply in a gusty wind.

In the absence of the raucous scrub jays, which have fled to an oak motte farther west, I seem, for a moment at least, to be alone. But as I sit here, my open journal resting on my lap, crickets begin chirping in the field at my back. Tiny red ants follow a trail from their nest, across the binoculars I've left lying on the ground, and into a pile of leaves. A single monarch butterfly floats across the road.

Here, in the middle of this hardscrabble Hill Country ranch, life shows itself in increments—in the beetle skittering across the rocks; in the clump of purple eryngo amid the dry, brown grass; in the silver-leaf nightshade's yellow fruit, lying plump and poisonous in the dust.

How suited each of these things is to its place, I think—rain lilies growing in the sandy soil along the road, white-winged doves disappearing into the brush, their wings whistling as they fly. Imagine this soil/air/water/light. Then imagine it filled with just these things. How appropriate it seems. How appropriate, and how good.

Can anything here, I wonder, imagine that it is filling a niche in the world? Can it know that outside this biome, this ecological system defined by weather and land form, it would be an altogether different thing? Can it know it might not be at all?

I am certain that it can't.

No, this beetle, this live oak, this clump of flowers clinging to the rock—all these things are simply being themselves, rooted to their place, thriving because they are so well suited to their task of living where they are.

What is my place? I wonder as I sit here on the side of the road. Brushing an ant from my leg, I imagine how one goes about finding a niche in the world, and how one claims it for herself. After nearly twenty years of teaching, and almost as many years of sitting at a desk, stringing words together on the page, I suppose that I should know the answer to such things.

I don't.

A mile or so down the road, the students I have brought here are finally beginning to stir. Having gotten up to watch the sunrise, they returned to bed to sleep several hours more. At 9:45 on this Saturday morning, they move slowly, tentatively, dragging themselves to the kitchen or to the screened-in porch one at a time.

What their songs and their words and their faces tell me, quite simply, is this: They, too, are looking for their places in the world. They, too, have a will to sink their roots into this rocky soil, to hang tight in the wind, to grow into their young and supple lives.

I wish I could tell them how.

It is mid-afternoon when nine of us climb into a truck, drive to the other side of the ranch, and come to a place called the Narrows. Grabbing towels and water bottles, we descend a set of rock steps leading from scrubby pasture land to the Little Blanco River forty feet below.

Dotted with miniature tinajas or pools, the limestone riverbed rolls out smooth and white before us, contained by the porous canyon walls. In reality, the rock here is a dull, gunmetal gray, but layered as it is in silt, it has a soft and doughy look, like yeast bread rising, lumpy in the sun.

Because I've forgotten my swimsuit, I will sit here while the others make their way upstream. Paddling, wading, scrambling over rocks, the students will stay in my sight for a minute. And then, trailing echoes of laughter as they round the curve of a cliff, they will disappear, leaving me alone with the trill of a canyon wren.

"Do you mind?" one of them asked before going.

"Not at all," I replied. And I was telling him the truth.

Opening my campstool in the shade, I sit for a moment, just listening for what there is to hear. Like the liquid wren song spilling from the sycamore's crown, water trickles from the rocks, dripping to the ground in shallow pools. Here and there, behind great boulders and next to the walls of the cliffs, water seems to seep out of the spongy earth. In such moist places, maidenhair ferns and river ferns abound, poison ivy clings to the gritty rocks, buttonbush and clumps of purple ironweed bloom.

It's all about knowing your place, it seems, about knowing what you need and what you can do without. It's all about knowing what it takes to live your life.

I am sitting on a pillow of rock, staring at minnows in a tiny pool, when the sound of voices comes filtering down the canyon. The students are on their way back. For the rest of the evening and into the moonlit night, they will talk about what they saw, about how every turn in the river offered them something new, about how every view was better than the last.

Listening to the students' adventures, I will think back to those minnows in their little ponds. Darting through isolated pools of water, they will flourish for a time, then die. Cut off from their source, from what they need to live, they will simply cease to be.

I will think, too, of the cliché I've heard so many times before.

"Bloom where you're planted," the posters of the sixties told us. But appealing as this sounds, it isn't how things work.

The buttonbush growing by the spring-fed pool, the purple eryngo thriving in the arid field—each blooms because it has the things it needs. Each flourishes because its place is right.

How do we know our place? I wonder as the students drift off sleepily to bed. Imagining the landscape of my life, I listen for the sound of roots taking hold, of leaves unfolding underneath the stars.

Personal Space and the
Mysteries of the Universe

S TANDING AT THE EDGE of the deck, my husband scans the tree tops for the first signs of a promised thunderstorm. There is the faint outline of a cloud bank some distance to the north, but otherwise the sky is remarkably clear.

He seems vaguely disappointed.

"The Big Dipper is tipped tonight," he says at last, casually changing the subject. He knows that out of a heaven full of stars, it is the only constellation I can recognize without a map.

"So, can you find the Dip Star?" I ask, teasing him with the term our daughter invented many years ago. In the glow of the television shining through the back window, I can see that my question has raised a smile.

A moment later, without saying a word, he pulls up one of the wrought iron patio chairs and sits, stretching his legs out in front of him.

"You know," he finally says, nodding toward the sky, "some of those stars may not even be there any more. That's really strange to think about."

And so it is.

Staring into the darkness of space, I am hard-pressed to imagine the distance to our own moon, much less to any of the one hundred billion stars that comprise the Milky Way. I can read that Alpha Centauri is 4.3 light years away, but how does the mind begin to fathom twenty-six trillion miles?

To be honest, I have no trouble understanding those who once believed that earth was the center of the universe. Sitting here on my deck, I am more than content to imagine that this yard, this clump of trees, this gray cat curled up at my feet—indeed, that all the givens of my life—are fixed points around which the rest of the cosmos whirls.

Intellectually, I know that our solar system is part of a vast collection of stars, gas, and dust stretching one hundred thousand light years through space. Intellectually, I can picture a swirling oval disc ten thousand light years thick, a disc so immense that it takes roughly two hundred million years to make a single revolution.

Intellectually, I have some sense of how the universe works, but sitting here on my deck, I am lost in a wave of stars.

On such a night, it is easy to imagine that gravity will fail at any moment, that in our weightless state we will rise toward the tree tops and simply float away in space. It is easy to imagine that after all these years, we can finally feel the earth spinning at a thousand miles an hour, that if we listen, we can hear the wind whistling in our ears.

Here in our suburban neighborhood, roughly six miles south of town, it is still possible to sit outside at night and see the stars burning overhead. It is still possible to imagine oneself whirling through the cosmos, to sense the limitlessness of space.

Grasping the arms of my chair, I hang on for a wild galactic ride.

Later, in the brightness of my living room, or the glare of my neighbor's floodlight, such thoughts will sound foolish indeed. Sitting in the glow of the television set, I will be reminded that the "real" world is a small and dangerous place, that there is evil lurking everywhere in the dark. No longer weightless, I will rise slowly and lock my doors and windows against the night.

Having spent much of my life outside the limits of any town, I can't imagine what it would be like to live today in one of America's inner cities. Lying in bed at night, listening to the chuck-will's-widow calling in the tree outside my window, I simply can't imagine coping with that much noise and light.

I would adapt, I suppose, but at what price?

Sitting on my deck on a clear summer night, I am reminded that regardless of the work piling up on my desk or the news blaring from the television set, the universe is larger than I can ever comprehend. I am reminded that time and speed are relative, that what I perceive as starlight may be the sunlight of another world.

The earth is a dangerous place, all right, but in the larger picture, it is also miraculously safe.

Looking for the Fire

THE IMAGE OF St. Francis sits on a tilting metal base, leaning back a bit and listing to the left. Cracked and glued together again, his is a crude concrete sculpture, pebbles showing at every seam. Rough cement has been smeared across his back, a reinforcement I suppose. A cobweb hangs loosely from his brow, winding past his elbow and waving out behind him like a thread unraveled from his sleeve. Gazing down at the nondescript bird perched on his forearm, this St. Francis looks much the worse for wear.

Sainthood, one must conclude, is never easy.

I am sitting near the end of a road or, more accurately, at the end of a wide, grassy path that stretches east from the center of camp. Past the baseball field, past the chapel, past the remnants of an ancient fence—in my twenty-five years of coming to this place, I have never walked this far, have never seen the listing statue of St. Francis or seen the river from this spot.

Days after a heavy rain fell to the north of here, the Guadalupe still shows the signs of flood. It is running more slowly now, but lower down from where I sit, the banks are covered with debris, and the ground is a slick, leaf-covered clay.

Save for the chirp of crickets and the sound of a basketball bouncing in the distance, the afternoon is quiet. Far behind me, beyond the deer pasture deep in knee-high golden grass, a car passes on the narrow country road. When it's gone, there is only the sound of the wind again and the creak of a tall pecan.

Sitting with my back against a tree, my legs outstretched atop a bed of cedar elm and hackberry leaves, I take a series of deep, deliberate breaths, inhaling the charged air of fall. Suddenly, a gunshot echoes from across the river. It is the first day of deer hunting season. It is the first day of the rest of my life, I think, appalled that this slogan of the sixties comes so easily to mind.

When the wind picks up, stinging my ears with its chill, I pull up the hood of my shirt and glance at the pile of books in my lap. I have escaped, it seems, escaped the steady hum of conversation, the steady drum, drum, drum of others' words against my brain.

Does this mean I'm antisocial? Reclusive? I'm inclined to think it does.

Picking up my copy of Mary Oliver's *White Pine*, I have a powerful urge to read her poetry aloud. I would like to recite her lines to the Spanish moss, to the deer hiding in the brush, to the green and sluggish river. St. Francis may have preached to the birds, but I am more reticent than he. Today, I mutter only to myself.

Looking at my watch, I see that twenty minutes have passed since I arrived at this place. Or is it my entire life? Fifty feet away from me stands the vestige of a once tall tree, its bark hanging off the trunk in sheets. I can see it, can trace it with my eyes, my hands, but can I know it? Like this presence that surrounds me, its essence somehow eludes. In its treeness, it refuses to be owned.

"I wish I knew the names of all the trees," one of the students had said to me today at lunch. "My father is a forester, and he used to tell me what they were."

I, too, have longed to know the names of things, but even more, I want to know the things.

Would I be surprised if, looking at the lanky pecan in front of me, I suddenly peered into its cambium, or if I saw bands of purple light instead of bark? Would I be surprised if, listening to the chirp of crickets, I suddenly heard the universe tilting or the stars keening in a galaxy far beyond our own?

Why can't I taste the wind? I wonder. *Feel the singing of birds against my skin? See the scent of fresh-cut autumn grass?* This is how I want to know the world, I remind myself. This is how I want to live.

Sometimes, when I lose my bearings, when I no longer know nor care where I am on the map or on the clock, I imagine I can do these things. Sometimes—just sometimes—I am fully conscious, wide awake.

It is November, and the world is ablaze with the blue light of autumn. Sleepers all, we walk through a forest of flaming trees, dreaming of what we will have for lunch.

In truth, the forest is very much on fire.

Jarred by the drone of a chain saw somewhere downstream, I look up as first one pecan leaf and then another lands on my blue-jeaned legs. A good sixty feet above me, a squirrel is foraging in the top of the tree for nuts, oblivious to my presence.

And to what am I oblivious? Our brother the sun, St. Francis called it. Our sister water, our brother fire, our mother the earth. Fellow creatures all, they were indeed his kin. So what are they to me?

"Humankind cannot bear very much reality." Again I remember those words.

Plucking a stem of autumn grass, I brush its feathered head against my hand, unsurprised by its softness. Had I keener vision, I would have seen the flames.

Simple Thoughts about
Having Enough

SITTING LESS THAN FIFTY FEET from the side of my house, behind a wall of native honeysuckle and jasmine and oak, I am invisible to the world. High above me, a puff of wind stirs the tops of the hackberries and elms, sending a wave of golden leaves cascading to the ground. They hit the earth like rain.

In this miniature wood adjacent to my house, this acre of live oak and cedar, persimmon and evergreen sumac, I delight in making lists. Indeed, for many years now I have watched this patch of ground go dormant every fall and renew itself each spring. And for most of those years, I have kept a running inventory of the place.

There's the single aromatic sumac not far from the mustang grape, the elbowbush and Indian currant, myrtle and mountain laurel, Mexican buckeye and red buckeye, beautyberry and anacua, littleleaf mulberry and Spanish oak, the agarita and the clump of yucca near that empty armadillo hole.

Here and there, charred stumps remind me that at one time this was open range. Today, however, it is home to chickadees and titmice, cardinals and ruby-crowned kinglets, blue jays and yellow-rumped warblers.

Small as it is, this wood is a world suffused with life.

Balanced on a weather-polished log, book resting in my lap, I pick up a twig and begin scratching idly through the leaves. How long, I wonder, have they been piling up this way? How long, I wonder, has this little world been building on itself?

Still damp from recent rains, and the luxury of constant shade, the leaves in the upper layer are pressed together like a mat. Prying it up with my twig, I lift a tiny section, hold it between finger and thumb, and contemplate the years it represents.

Leaves turning to leaf mold turning to soil—what could be richer than the floor of a forest in the fall? And who could be richer than I—sitting on this log, under this blue sky, in the coolness of this autumn afternoon?

"Increasingly," I wrote to a friend not long ago, "my house is being filled with bits and pieces of the world." Was it the clutch of bird feathers on the butcher block table that told me this? The chips of copper ore and hematite on the shelf above the pewter? The "special rock"—a gift from a thoughtful godchild—on the bedroom dresser by the clock? It was each of these and more.

Because, like most people, I am conscious just a fraction of the time, I quite frequently forget how very rich I am. These bits of earth remind me of that fact.

"This is not a Third World problem," a friend of mine is fond of saying in response to things that cause her stress. So the dog needs medication for his thyroid? Two of the family's three cars are in the shop? The VCR is on the blink? Inconveniences, yes; worries, yes, but hardly Third World problems, my friend would say. It's time to get a grip.

So how much is enough? I ask myself from time to time. *How much stuff do I really need?* In a world where stuff means security and power, status and love, it seems impossible to have too much. And yet, when I listen to my heart, I know that real wealth lies somewhere else.

Sitting on this log in this little wood, I consider the true richness of my life. What is it that brings me joy and peace and a sense that this life is good?

Opening the book on my lap, I read the words of David Whyte, who writes in *The Heart Aroused*, "Having an elemental and intimate relationship with the things of the world instead of wishing to possess them gives us a home at the center of life that is already furnished and paid for."

The thought is simple, and yet it has the clarity and weight of truth. Here in the chill of an autumn afternoon, in the rustle of leaves and the musky scent of soil, in the circle of friends and family, in this meeting of heaven and earth—here, I know, I am given everything I need.

Gills

OCTOBER 11: It has been raining now for days. First as a gentle mist and then a deluge, a nonstop pounding on the metal roof, the autumn storm has wrapped around us like the sea. Walking to the mailbox or running from the front porch to the car, we imagine earth reverting to some primeval state. We imagine ourselves evolving backwards, settling into the ooze.

We contemplate the need for gills.

Still, after weeks of hot, dry weather—after watching the world around me bake and then shut down—I am surprised to see what days of unrelenting rain can do. Surprised to find these whorls of green, these tender stems, these pairs of perfect leaves, I am—more than anything—surprised to see the earth is very much alive.

"It's amazing what difference some water makes," my husband says as we stand together on the drive. Having brought him out to look at what I've just discovered in the once-bare soil, I point to the oval, waxy leaves of next spring's bluebonnets, to the small sprigs of green that dot the spongy ground.

Not there a week ago, they've suddenly appeared. Inventing themselves, coaxed by water and light from darkness underground, they have sprouted overnight. They have willed themselves to life.

Everywhere, lying atop the soil or buried out of sight, seeds wait silently for cues, for signals that the time, the temperature, the air is right. And then, as if responding to the magnetism of the sun, they split, burst open, stretch their thin green tendrils toward the light.

Winged seeds, seeds in cases, seeds with edges sharp as spears—millions of them lie waiting for the moment they will come to life. Hackberries and sumac, salvia and penstemon, zexmenia and sunflower goldeneye—species upon species wait to populate the earth.

"The extravagant gesture is the stuff of creation," Annie Dillard has written. And what, I wonder, is more extravagant than this? Autumn, I realize, is every bit as profligate as spring.

OCTOBER 16: When the rain is ended and the sun is shining in a chilly autumn sky, I gather up my tools and head out to the front yard to dig. Intent on grubbing out a wayward patch of grass, I will almost miss the fact that tiny seedlings—gaillardias perhaps?—already dot the sandy soil. I will almost miss the fact that life, small as it is, has chosen to return.

In *The Desert Year*, Joseph Wood Krutch writes of what may be one of the most intriguing creatures of the Sonoran Desert, where he lived the last part of his life—the spadefoot toad. Living underground most of the year, the Sonoran spadefoot (*Scaphiopus couchi*) erupts from the earth following the first good summer rain, breeds, lays its eggs in a puddle of water, and disappears again.

For Krutch, witnessing this phenomenon held more mysteries than it solved. "How much of the time does he remain buried?" Krutch wondered of the toad. "Does he come out to eat occasionally during the almost year-long period when he is rarely if ever seen? Finally, how does he like the extraordinary existence which he seems to lead?"

Reading Krutch's words, I imagine how such a resurrection scene must look. Never having met a spadefoot toad, I can only recall the experience I once had of driving down the interstate at night in a dreadful summer storm. Inches deep in water, the highway was also—or so it seemed—inches deep in frogs. Whether washed onto the blacktop by the heavy rain or there by choice, amphibians erupted from the road like popcorn, scattering in the headlights of the car.

Hours later, they were gone.

What power is it, I wonder, that triggers such unlikely bursts of life? What moves the seemingly inert to resurrect itself, to stretch its legs/limbs/leaves inexplicably and gladly toward the sun?

Does it move in me as well?

OCTOBER 21: Lying on the still-green lawn, hands locked and resting underneath my head, I watch as a bank of steel gray clouds rolls in across the tree line to the north. I catch the scent of autumn on the breeze, the scent of changes in the wind. And just beneath me, I imagine, a world is waiting to be born.

Homeland Security
Safe at Home in the World

IT IS MORNING as I walk along the bare caliche road, as my sandals crunch across the gravel, drowning out the mid-September songs of birds.

It is morning when suddenly it occurs to me that, for reasons unexplained, I am not being struck by lightning. I am not falling into a crevice and disappearing into the earth. I am not bursting into flames or whirling into space. My body is intact.

It is a morning in mid-September when I wonder why it is that I so seldom marvel at the fact that I'm alive. Why does it seem so ordinary to be occupying time and space?

I hold out my hand and see the veins, see the knuckles, tendons rippling underneath the skin. I see the tiny scar there on my middle finger where I accidentally burned it as a child, the callous where I gripped the pruning shears too long.

What is it, I wonder, that tells my hand to brush the bangs out of my eyes, that tells my fingers to adjust the glasses riding down my nose, that tells my feet to rise and fall, rise and fall in a rhythm that makes sense?

As a rule, I must admit, I am not moved by mysteries such as this. And yet, this morning I am baffled by them all. This morning, for an instant at least, I am fully in my body, fully in my life. My feet are on the ground. I am, as some would put it, "placed."

Were I more literal-minded than I am, my curiosity would not be piqued by such phenomena as this. I would be satisfied to know, for instance, that it is some electric impulse coursing down the nervous pathway from my brain, some charge emitting from any of ten billion neurons causing me to stop on this caliche road, to bend over from the waist, to touch the flower of an Indian mallow in full bloom.

As it is, though, I'm confounded by the simplest of things.

Think about it: The earth is traveling through space at something like sixty-seven thousand miles an hour, the galaxy at more than 370 miles a second. Though I state these numbers as I might recite my zip code or my street address, I can fathom neither speed. Tell me that the average human body contains roughly fifty million million cells, that each of these cells contains six feet of chromatin—structures composed of DNA and protein—that any sequence of DNA in any complex of chromatin in any cell can go terribly, terribly wrong— wrong enough to kill. Tell me that my body is as vulnerable as this, and I will wonder how I've made it through a single day, much less the half century that I've lived.

And yet, the truth is this: no less than the elbowbush growing wild outside my study window or the white-winged doves cooing at sunset, no less than the armadillo that roots in my garden at night or the Gulf fritillary that flits across the blooming flame acanthus—no less than any of these, I am suited to this place. It is my home, my source. We are a perfect fit.

This doesn't mean, of course, that real dangers don't exist. A coral snake might be hiding in the leaves around my air conditioner, just as one was when the repairman last came to do some work. The mosquitoes that bite at my ankles and calves might carry West Nile virus, or encephalitis, or something more exotic; dengue fever, perhaps. The ground beneath our house might shift, leaving the foundation cracked and all the pipes askew. The weather might turn bad. Hail, lightning, floods, blue northers, tornadoes, ice—the possibilities for disaster are vast.

When I was growing up on the central Texas coast, for example, hurricanes were an indisputable part of life. Most of the time they skirted Bay City, where I lived, but in September of 1961, the strongest storm in forty years came inland across Matagorda Bay, the brunt of its power felt by the towns of Port O'Connor and Port Lavaca—only fifty miles away.

What were the odds of a major hurricane hitting so close to my hometown? In a typical year, fairly small. While tropical storms are endemic to the Texas coast, the chances of one becoming a hurricane and actually doing serious harm are between 3 and 4 percent.

I suppose it was simply our turn.

With steady winds of more than 150 miles an hour and an eye that stretched for thirty miles, Hurricane Carla was a Category 4 storm on the Saffir-Simpson five-point scale—extreme by any definition. Still the largest Texas storm on record, with its mix of hurricane and gale force winds cutting a swath five hundred miles wide, it produced storm tides of ten to twenty-two feet, left shrimp boats marooned on highways miles from any dock, swept up birds in the Yucatan and dropped them like hail on the Port Lavaca streets, or so some residents said. It spawned twenty-six tornadoes, removed eight hundred feet of Gulf shoreline from Matagorda Island, and cost forty-six people their lives, most by drowning.

Granted, there had been deadlier storms, such as the so-called West India Hurricane, the Great Storm that flooded Galveston in 1900, taking at least six thousand lives. There would be costlier storms as well, including Hurricane Celia in 1970. This storm, with its wind gusts of almost two hundred miles an hour, would result in nearly half a billion dollars in losses to property and crops—the equivalent of three billion dollars today. It would destroy close to nine thousand homes in the Corpus Christi area, with another fourteen thousand suffering major damage of some kind.

Yes, there had been worse storms, with a good many more to

come. But for me, Carla was unique: The life it affected was mine.

Just ten years old at the time, I didn't know where to begin preparing for such an event. How long before the wind started, I wondered. Would our house be okay? Would we be okay?

Longing to do something, I rummaged through the kitchen drawers for a piece of string, went outside, and, under the gathering cover of gray, tied a newly planted live oak tree—our only tree—to the street sign a few feet away.

I truly believed it would help.

My parents, meanwhile, stocked up on bread and milk, bought extra batteries for the flashlights, filled the bathtub with water—and tried to prepare for the worst.

Then, for as long as we could, the five of us—my brother, sister, parents, and I—watched a trenchcoat-clad Dan Rather broadcasting from the Galveston seawall. Gathered around our black-and-white TV, we sat enthralled by the sight of waves crashing over rocks, wind bending trees to the ground.

When the blackout came, my sister and brother and I went out to the garage and climbed into the front seat of my mother's 1957 Plymouth Fury. There we listened to the radio, periodically running back inside to give our parents the latest news.

The storm passed sometime in the night.

The next morning, with the water and power still off, we piled into my father's company car and headed downtown, where a single café was open and serving food. Coming and going, we gawked at the fallen trees, at the piles of limbs and other debris strewn across people's lawns. Among the lucky ones, we had lost only five shingles from the roof of our newly constructed house. To my parents' great surprise, the live oak had survived as well.

More than forty years after this storm, I live on the Balcones Fault, the part of Central Texas where the Coastal Plain and the Edwards Plateau intersect. With its spring-fed rivers, limestone canyons, and oak-covered hills, it is among the most beautiful places on earth. It is also among the most dangerous.

Thanks to rapid runoff and the tendency for large storms to stall here for several days, no area in the United States is more prone to major flash flooding than the Balcones Escarpment of Texas. In late June of 2002, for example, as much as two to three feet of rain fell in only a matter of days. At Canyon Lake, roughly twenty-five miles to the west, the lake level rose forty feet, coming over the spillway for the first time since the dam was completed in 1966. In the nearby community of Sattler, where flood stage on the Guadalupe River is only nine feet, the water crested at thirty-seven feet.

The upshot of all this? The earth is a dangerous place.

As a person whose house has been struck by lightning and whose bedroom window has been smashed by tornadic winds, I should probably be very afraid. Knowing what I know—not only about weather but also about rattlesnakes hiding under logs and brown recluse spiders nesting in people's shoes—I should probably shudder at the hazards of being alive.

I think of this now as I check the headlines or watch the evening news: earthquake in Algeria, SARS in China, tornadoes in Missouri and Kansas. Anxiety levels are high.

As much as we fear such natural processes, however, we fear ourselves even more. The threat of attack by terrorists is high, we're warned; the nation is on orange alert. As a result, citizens should be wary of anyone behaving in an odd or suspicious way. Assume that weapons of mass destruction, including those containing chemical, biological, or radiological agents, are being readied for attack. Though we can't know where or when, trust that terrorists are at this very moment planning to wreak havoc at a public event near you. Remember that the enemy is no one and everyone, that the danger, though amorphous, is real; it is like the air you breathe. Know that people with more information than you have are convinced that the worst is possible—if not today, then tomorrow, or maybe a week from now.

The message? The world is out to get you. Be afraid.

Like many of my friends, I find little reassurance in the color-coded warnings or the airport screenings or the presence of men with guns. The threat is too fuzzy for these to appease my fears. The times are dangerous, we are told repeatedly. Take care. Watch out. But watch for what, we ask?

Life is out to get you. Be afraid.

Lying awake in the dark, I spent countless childhood nights imagining the way the world would end. First there would be a burnt orange glow on the horizon, then a blinding light, then the cloud. It could happen any night, I continually reminded myself. It would surely happen at night.

My fears were stoked not only by my choice of reading material—books such as Nevil Shute's *On the Beach*—but also by the duck-and-cover drills we did at school, by the fallout shelter frenzy, by images of a somber JFK addressing the nation and a maniacal Khrushchev banging his shoe on the table to drive a point home. "We will bury you!" he warned us in 1956. His words hung in the air like smoke.

The atmosphere is much the same today. But with roughly nineteen million Americans suffering from an anxiety disorder of some kind, we're now learning the price of our fear. We are learning the damage that hypervigilance can do.

Should we be concerned about possible terrorist threats? Only the very naive would say that the danger's not real. There are malevolent forces at work to destroy the things we hold dear. There is evil in the world. There are cruelty and anger and misuse of power. There are arrogance, intolerance, and greed.

I can't deny these exist.

At the same time, though, I can't live a life fed by fear. Just as I can't go to bed every night imagining a nuclear blast or a tornado tearing off my roof, I can't begin every day envisioning the worst things that people can do; I can't survive in a world where stopping to rest, to breathe, to be caught off guard, is seen as a perilous act.

So for me, the question is this: How do we live with the fear, with the awful awareness that we are indeed vulnerable creatures, that we face a risk that is real?

What the earth tells me is that the question isn't new. There has always been an inherent threat in simply being alive. A single-celled organism can fell even the strongest among us; a hundred-year flood or a tornado at just the wrong time can wipe a community out. People do lose their lives. In the mathematics of mortality, it's the way the universe works.

And yet, for all the precariousness of flesh, we are fundamentally safe here on earth. Given all that could go wrong—tsunamis washing away our homes, sinkholes opening under our feet, asteroids crashing on our heads—it's worth noting that such disasters are simply not the norm: they're still considered news.

There is, then, a kind of holding-in-tension that I am trying to learn. In this both/and way of looking at the world, security lies somewhere between the knowledge of our own fragility and our sense that we are at home here. To live with both truths is not to deny our fears but to see them as part of the whole. Life and not-life, hope and not-hope—the capacity for paradox is what saves us.

"In this wilderness I have learned how to sleep again," Thomas Merton wrote in *Raids on the Unspeakable.* "I am not alien. The trees I know, the night I know, the rain I know. I close my eyes and instantly sink into the whole rainy world of which I am a part, and the world goes on with me in it, for I am not alien to it."

Several years ago, a friend who had been seriously ill wrote to tell me of the changes in her life. "I have the sense that I'm being distilled," she explained, "simplified by forces I can't name."

The process, she added, was less disturbing than it seemed. It was, in fact, a little bit like being on the bottom of the pool, or underwater in a lake, looking up and seeing the turbulence on top but not being battered by the waves.

When I read this, I felt myself swept back to the afternoon fifteen months before, when having crashed into a massive rock, two friends and I were thrown from our canoe. While they managed to cling to the fallen pecan tree partially blocking our way, I was swept beneath it, pinned down by the swirling current.

At first I was simply surprised. We had made a mistake, I realized; we could certainly make it right. But then the panic set in. Struggling to grab hold of the tree, I fought the weight of the water, fought the force that was pulling me down. *This doesn't happen to me,* I protested. But it *was* me, and I knew I was going to drown.

Life and not-life, hope and not-hope. In a split second, my world became quiet and still. With the sky a mere shaft of light above me, a blue glow in the midafternoon, I felt the fear slip away like a skin. For that moment, for just a moment, I felt safe. Living or dying, I was going to be okay.

Living it would be. Washed up on a gravel bar, I had dragged myself to a nearby rock, had sat there staring at my hands. What struck me then, what struck me later as I read the letter from my friend, was just how strange it was to be alive. Moved by the fact that I was still in my body, I had come out of the river knowing something that I hadn't known before. I had learned how thin the margin between life and death really is. I had learned a little bit of letting go, of letting myself be borne away by something I could neither understand nor tame. I had learned to trust my own life.

"Everything is distilled," I told my friend, recalling the events of the summer before. It's distilled to something that feels like a single pebble or a single grain of sand or a single drop of water, and you know this something is your life. For an instant, you hold it in your hands or taste it on your lips, but then, quite suddenly, it's gone.

Walking along a rough caliche road in mid-September, a woman is jolted by the mental image of herself alone on a gravel bar, staring in amazement at her empty hands. This is your life, the stones in the river tell her. Pick it up and hold it lightly; turn it over and over; let it go. Let it gently fall into the flow of the river. Let it be carried away like sand. Let it disappear from sight, becoming a part of the current as it goes. Let it not matter any longer that you have lost it. Let the losing of it set you free.

Walking with the wind against her back, with the sun on the side of her face and the sound of crunching gravel underneath her feet, the woman is grounded in this time and in this place. She knows that the world is dangerous, that life is dangerous, but she also loves the way her body feels as it travels across the earth. Holding both hope and fear in her heart, she is, she knows, safe at home.

Experiencing the Fall

IT IS FOUR or three or perhaps not quite noon. I've lost all track of time here on this gray, bone-chilling afternoon. Sitting on a hollow tree stump, running my hand through the Labrador's thick fur, I am lulled by the roar of the Guadalupe, lulled by the rush of a river tumbling briskly over rocks.

Suddenly, from somewhere in the distance, comes the muffled pop of a hunter's gun, then the echo of a car door being slammed. High above me, Spanish moss hangs limply in the trees, gray-green, like tattered lace. Sounds and colors, textures and shapes—all is muted, seemingly subdued this time of year.

Later, as I sit on a porch swing half a mile away, these images replay themselves upon the blank screen of my mind. Yellow-blooming horseherb lying flush against the rain-soaked ground, a pair of white-tailed deer grazing peacefully on the lawn, voices murmuring like water just beyond the window—moment by moment, the day invents itself, takes flesh, begins to breathe.

Sitting on this porch swing, a sleeping cat compactly curled up in my lap, I feel the pulsing rhythm of the world.

It is the first weekend in November. Another fall, another layer peeled away.

"This is the thinnest season," a friend writes, using terminology she has borrowed from the Celts. Perceived only faintly in other months, strong presences abound. Diaphanous as light, the veil between the real and Real is wearing down to air. I breathe, and hear it giving way.

Here in the Texas Hill Country, far from the noise of the class-room and the din of the ringing phone, it is easy to discern such change. Press your hand against the sky and see the imprint of your ruddy palm. Walk lightly on the muddy earth and hear it sing. Brush past the brittle grama grass and feel it burn.

As astronomer Chet Raymo suggests in "The Blandishments of Color," November is the season "when the eye must pay close atten-tion." Color, if it comes at all, is nothing more than a flash: the cap of a ruby-crowned kinglet, a single clump of ripe beautyberries dangling from a branch, the golden leaves of a cedar elm, here and gone in a matter of days—we enjoy each one as a glimpse.

If I am still enough and quiet, if I am keen enough in looking at the world, will it catch fire, blaze, reduce itself to flame? Or will it simply disappear like glass, transparent, clean?

In this season of subtraction, in this time of waxing nights and waning days, the meanings of things lie just below the surface, just beyond the thin veneer of thought. Wipe that thought away, like con-densation on a window, and we see the wonder of the world shine through.

It is a night in early November, and I am riding into town with my husband. An hour or so past dark, the sky is nonetheless glowing, thanks to the light of a bright, white moon.

"Take a look," I tell him when we get beyond the ragged row of trees. "Doesn't the moon look good?"

Full, or very nearly so, the moon hangs high above the empty pas-ture at the bottom of our hill. Around it shines a band of milky light. This halo effect, a physicist friend later tells me, is caused by water droplets in our atmosphere. Also known as a corona or aureole, this relatively narrow ring is formed by a process called diffraction. Though much more common than the larger colored rings that show up only three or four times a winter, this phenomenon is no less wondrous, no less grand.

"Wasn't it lovely?" my physicist friend remarks, having explained just how it came to be. Even after all his years of staring at the heavens, his years of studying the moon, he hasn't lost the will to be amazed.

Lengthening nights and waning days, simplicity of earth as it moves toward black and white, toward the thinnest of seasons, there is much to love about the world, and much that brings delight.

The World of Sense

Ucks," my husband whispers, nudging my elbow with his hand. Moving ahead a foot or so, I see them—first the female, rising from the creek where they've been feeding, and then the male, green, luminescent, unmistakable even in flight.

"Wood ducks," I say, half fearing to name what is right before my eyes. They are the first such birds I've ever seen. And with a single cry of alarm, they are gone.

Exchanging few words, my husband and I sit cross-legged in the grass, high above the little creek. If we are very still, we imagine, the ducks will return. Or the fox he spotted here yesterday, its nose to the earth as it trotted by the water's edge, will magically reappear.

We wait, saying nothing, seeing nothing but the glint of water as it swirls past the skull of a long-dead buck and gently falls across a lip of rock. We wait, and we watch, and at last we shrug and stiffly pull ourselves up from the ground.

By now, we admit, the ducks have headed for the river, found some quiet pool beneath some other line of trees, and started feeding in the shallows off some other muddy bank. They will not be coming back.

Brushing the leaves from our pants, we push through a brittle stand of frostweed and make our way back toward the broken fence. Beyond it, a deer pasture stretches out, golden even in the winter mist.

It is two days after New Year's, and my husband and I are spending the weekend in a cottage at the far end of this field. Without agendas, we have eased into the rhythm of the place. We have read, we have slept, we have listened as the wind moved through the trees. And now, with a hint of rain in the air and the sound of snapping branches at our feet, we walk.

We enter the world of sense.

Spotting a deer track, my husband slips through the sagging fence and heads north toward the creek. Close behind, I stop and call him back, believing I've found a small dead bird caught on a rusty wire.

What looks to be a feathered body, however, turns out to be an open milkweed pod, dangling from a stiff, dry stem. Mottled like the tawny back of a Carolina wren, the pod is filled with tufts of creamy down. At the end of each is a flat, brown seed, elliptical and taut.

It is a live thing I am holding in my hand, a live thing born of earth and rain and sun. Surprised by its lightness, I take it with me when we go.

"Another treasure?" my husband says, smiling as we make our way along the fence. Amused by my penchant for collecting, for gathering yaupon berries and pecans and clumps of Spanish moss, he knows the answer long before I speak.

"Yes," I tell him, secretly pleased that he has seen.

Skirting the edge of the woods, we pause to watch a rock squirrel disappear into its hole. "I guess they're not as curious as marmots," my husband says when the creature fails to reappear. "He must not want to know who's watching him up here."

Feeding in a pool where the river intersects the creek, a trio of carp prove to be less shy. While two of them dart after bubbles, the third and largest of the group begins to work itself into the mud. Like a blunt instrument ramming the bottom, it sends up a cloud of silt with every strike.

"I'm going to stay a while," I tell my husband, who has started to move away. Letting him leave to search for birds, I head farther down the river, where I stop to watch another rock squirrel running through the brush.

It is here that the words of Mary Oliver's poem "Wild Geese" begin playing in my head. "You do not have to be good," she opens. It is the only line of the poem that I know by heart. I suspect it is enough.

"You do not have to be good." Looking around me, I know that I am part of everything I see; I know that I belong. I know this not because I have earned it, not because I have worked hard, not because I am good—but simply because I am.

"You do not have to walk on your knees / for a hundred miles through the desert, repenting. / You only have to let the soft animal of your body / love what it loves."

Three days into another year, I'm envisioning what it is I love. I'm envisioning the shape of kindness, imagining the subtle way it comes, the way it speaks our name, the way it gives us what we need.

Lying on the grass beside the river's edge, I listen as the titmice twitter in the trees behind my head. Above me, the naked branches of a large pecan spread out like thread-fine capillaries set against an ash gray sky.

Loving my own tired flesh, letting the world wrap around me like a second skin, I sink into the earth, let go, and breathe. There are many ways to be kind, I imagine, many ways to pay attention to our soft and supple lives.

A Preference for Winter

WHEN I "had my color done" many years ago, I discovered—hardly to my surprise—that I am a "winter." What this means, in practical terms, is that I supposedly look my best in dark, vivid colors—forest green, royal or navy blue, burgundy, black, and so on. Fortunately, these are colors I already tended to like.

While this system was obviously meant to focus on appearance alone, I have often found myself wondering if it has a corollary in the natural world. Could it be that some of us are winter people, while others are more in tune with summer or fall?

Granted, if I were asked to pick a single season as my own, I'd be hard-pressed to name just one.

For example, while summer has never been at the top of my list—it's too hot, too humid for my taste—I wouldn't be without its sheer opulence. At least until the annual drought sets in, it is the season of jewel-colored cosmos and zinnias sparkling along the edges of the lawn, of the scent of lemon grass bruised by the passing of a sleek gray cat, of cicadas singing in the shade of evening.

More to my liking, spring is the season of surprise, of dew on the clover, of sudden storms and bees humming in the larkspur.

Autumn, in contrast, is almost painfully perfect. Tipped just so, the earth is bathed in lapis sky, sprayed by a final burst of red salvia and sunflower goldeneye. Unlike the Texas spring, which often begins early and ends late, fall may well exhaust itself in a single afternoon. Crisp and sweet, it hangs lightly in the imagination, recalling sunlight spilling through an open window, or children laughing in a pile of spent leaves.

"I don't know which to prefer," poet Wallace Stevens writes in "Thirteen Ways of Looking at a Blackbird,"

> *The beauty of inflections*
> *Or the beauty of innuendoes,*
> *The blackbird whistling*
> *Or just after.*

To prefer the beauty of fall is to prefer the intensity of memory, the ache of sudden loss. It is to choose the lingering scent of cedar rather than the flame. Because it is perfect, and therefore transitory, autumn vanishes the moment it is apprehended. Were it not for that, were it not for the chill its absence leaves, my preference would no doubt be for fall.

Am I a "winter person," then, only by default? I have considered the possibility—and rejected it.

If fall is the sound of music remembered after the note has been struck, winter is the silence that follows. It is, essentially, a time of waiting, of letting be.

Standing in my garden in mid-November, I sense that the earth is in the process of shutting down. Covering itself with leaves from the Spanish oak, from the crape myrtle and pistache, it grows quiet and still beneath my feet. Life is going underground.

More so than any season, winter is a time of paradox. Seemingly dead, the huisache spends the long night rejuvenating itself, sending its roots into the dark and fertile soil. Phlox seeds, dropped in the heat of summer, sprout anonymously amid the tired refuse of autumn.

"Love winter when the plant says nothing," Thomas Merton writes. To love winter, it would seem, is to love the fact that what we see and what we know are only a portion of what is. It is to love the hiddenness of things, to love them in their incompleteness and in their growth.

Kneeling in my garden, only weeks away from winter, I brush the leaves from the damp soil, take a scoop of it in my bare hand, and find it full of earthworms. Slowly, silently, they are reinventing the world.

Naming Day

A T FIRST I IMAGINE it is an agitated squirrel barking at me
from the trees, but there is none of the usual follow-up, no
chatter, no *chk-chk-chk* to frighten me away. Looking up, I
quickly discover that I am being watched not by a squirrel but by a
black vulture perched in the top of a leafless elm.

Woof, it calls again, opening its mouth afterward in what appears to
be a yawn. *Woof.* Turning its head, it looks around, stretching first one
taloned foot and then the other. Portrait of a vulture in repose.

Perhaps it's my imagination, but thanks to the shifting breeze, I
catch the smell of something not quite living, something hidden in
the tangle of grass and grape vines and possumhaw at my back. Perhaps this vulture sees me not just as an intruder but as competition for
its midday meal.

I am considering this possibility when, quite suddenly, I hear
another *woof* and the flutter of giant wings. The big bird glides down
from its perch, flies over me, and floats across the water to the woods
beyond. Now it is just me and the chickadees, me and the trilling
wren, the titmice, and the river spilling over the rocks below.

Here on the third day of Christmas, in the chill and solace of a
damp December wood, I am celebrating the season—again. Two
mornings before, there had been carols coming from the stereo, coffee
brewing in the kitchen, presents unwrapped and piled beneath the

tree. Today, however, there is none of that. Today there is only the gray of a winter sky, the silence of leaves, the hum of water washing over cypress knees.

It is all the gift I need.

I have come to this place because I am tired and I want to get away. After a busy semester of teaching, of writing, of doing, I am ready just to be. And so, for two nights and three days, I will retreat here, cooking my simple meals in the kitchen of a renovated farmhouse, reading and drinking tea in a comfortable chair, sleeping as long as I like.

But it will not be enough.

Inevitably, something will draw me outside, will pull me down this path to the river, where I will sit beneath a naked cedar elm for hours at a time. Why, I will wonder, have I chosen to come here?

Laying my binoculars down for a moment, I recall the words of Thoreau, who said that he went to the woods because he wished to "live deliberately," to "front only the essential facts of life." But I am no Thoreau. My reasons are more elementary yet.

I am here, my weary mind tells me, to be surrounded by things I cannot understand, by creatures I can glimpse but not possess. I am here to watch the leaves decay, to listen to the river utter sounds that have no meaning for my ears. I am here to be gawked at by the birds, to be seen as the interloper that I am.

I am here to peer into hollow trees, to be startled by the red of possumhaw berries against the gray of a winter wood. I am here to feel the damp earth beneath my jeans, the roughness of the cedar elm against my back.

Imagining that I am here to find my self, I suddenly realize this isn't true at all. I am here, instead, to pare away, to name all I am not. I am here, most certainly, to forget. And to remember.

Touching the moist earth, working my fingers through the layers of elm and cypress leaves, I find the rich humus that lies not far below. Hidden, it comes to its life in the dark. Mute, it comes to its life without thought.

Breaking the silence, a cardinal calls from a brush pile just across the river. To my left, another answers. To my right, still another *chir-r-r-r-s* in response. Sounds swirl all around me, and I am dumb to know what they mean.

In the morning, turning as I walk along the river's rocky edge, I will catch a great blue heron taking flight. It will lift off silently, gliding across the water and up the bank beyond. I will watch it disappear. Finding a dry place to sit, I will watch the river become smaller and smaller, will wonder where it ends, where it begins.

And then, not satisfied, I will ask myself yet again—why have I come here?

Sitting under the cypress trees draped with Spanish moss, I will realize at last that it is ritual I've sought, some act to bring this old year, this old life to a close. And so, gathering twigs and leaves from atop the weathered rock, I will send them flying, one by one, into the current, naming them as they go. Deadlines, fears, anxieties of all kinds—taking the shape of cypress leaves, of bits of bark, of grass, they will drift on the flowing water, will be weightlessly borne away.

Here to name what I am not, I will sit on this bank and watch as wave after wave spills over the polished rock. Here to forget, to remember that my life is more than any total of its parts, I will let the river wrap around me like the songs of birds. I will feel its sound wash over me like grace.

Entering the Emptiness at Lebh Shomea

I AM ON a lonely road and I am traveling, traveling, traveling, traveling—looking for something, what can it be?"

Pulling up to the stop sign, I roll down the window, pop the scratchy Joni Mitchell tape out of the cassette player, and wait as a young man in a black tank top and jeans wanders toward the car with a clipboard in his hand.

"Afternoon," he says, squinting in the bright South Texas sun. "Your name?"

Scanning his list to see if I'm on it, he makes a mark by my name, walks around to the front of the car to get my license plate number, and waves me on, telling me to "have a nice stay."

Two miles of narrow asphalt road lie between this checkpoint and the community known as Lebh Shomea. Having spent the last five hours riding a wave of spring break traffic headed south, I am suddenly alone, suddenly aware that for the next seven days I am more or less on my own.

More or less, because in spite of the solitude and silence, no one is ever completely alone at Lebh Shomea. Guests eat meals family style in the basement dining room of the Big House, and everyone—including the handful who live and work there as hermits—is expected at the 7:00 A.M. Eucharist each day.

In short, running through the quiet of this place is a kind of pulse, an energy that draws in stranger and friend alike. I sense it as soon as I arrive.

"Have you been with us before?" Sister Maria had asked when I called in January to make my reservation. Hearing that this was my second visit to Lebh Shomea, which occupies roughly eleven hundred acres of scrub in the middle of the historic Kenedy Ranch, she told me that she'd leave my room assignment on the message board in the dining hall. For anyone already familiar with the place, picking up that assignment is all there is to checking in.

This spring break, I discover, I'll be staying in Joseph, one of the dozen or so private dwellings that form a compound behind the Big House. Like every other building and room at Lebh Shomea, a term which in Hebrew means "listening heart," it has been given a biblical name not only to make it easier to find but to remind the guests that this is no ordinary place.

Once the property of Sarita Kenedy East, granddaughter and heir of South Texas cattle baron Mifflin Kenedy, Lebh Shomea has served since 1973 as a wilderness for renewal and refuge, an oasis for study and discovery, a contemplative community and school of prayer. Operating under the auspices of the Missionary Oblates of Mary Immaculate, it is home to three core members—a priest and two nuns who spend a good part of their time writing, caring for the plants, maintaining the large library, planning meals, and tending to other necessary chores—and way station for a host of pilgrims, whose stay may be as short or as long as they please.

"Guests who wish to share our desert silence for indefinite periods are welcome year 'round," reads the brochure that is sent to prospective visitors. "There is no predetermined schedule, no imposed structure, only the freedom and creativity of solitude."

It is my first night at Lebh Shomea, and I am lying on my back on the east lawn, watching wind-driven clouds congealing overhead. One minute they are feathery soft like the dappled, downy underside of a goose. The next they are the skim on scalded milk, separating and drawing themselves together like cream. And behind them all, as they scud across the sky, shines the sure, steady presence of the moon.

"Although certain basic comforts are afforded—heating for cold winter northers and fans for sultry summer days—life at Lebh Shomea is always experienced with a certain aesthetic acceptance of the weather, hot or cold, wet or dry," reads a page in the notebook that sits on every visitor's desk. "To feel the cool evening breeze across one's body is refreshment that air conditioning can never quite match. We forgo the convenience of security lights on the property so that the stars can be seen in all their brilliance."

Their presumed emptiness aside, it is the nights at Lebh Shomea that I find most rich. The whinny of the screech owl, the *pur-WEEER* of the pauraque, the "purring" of the turkeys roosting in the trees outside my window, the *kerr-r-rock kerr-r-rock* of the spring's first frogs, the howling of coyotes drifting in across the fields—like the moon and stars, these also form a presence here, all the more compelling for their hiddenness.

"It's been an interesting experience," one of my tablemates reveals at the noon meal on Sunday, the only time of the week when conversation is allowed. "I'm not sure I'd wish it on my worst enemy." He is smiling when he tells me this, but there is a truth in his statement nonetheless.

The hardest thing about being here, he admits, is what he calls the "desert experience"—and he is not referring only to the cactus and the javelinas and the heat. "You have to face yourself," he says. After six months at Lebh Shomea, after six months of burrowing to bedrock, he should know.

Silence, Pico Iyer writes in "The Eloquent Sounds of Silence," could be said to be "the ultimate province of trust: it is the place where we trust ourselves to be alone; where we trust others to understand the things we do not say; where we trust a higher harmony to assert itself."

On another night, in another moment out beneath the stars, I lie and watch the full moon rise above the huisache and the palms. To trust this emptiness, I have discovered, is to hear it resonate with presence. To enter it, to let it wrap itself around me like dew, is finally to know that there is nothing left to say, and everything to learn.

Living Our Lives as Play

SEEKING SHELTER from the rain in this oak motte, I am become like the creatures around me. First it is one, then another, then a third black vulture I see heading home to roost in the motte adjacent to mine. Finally, wondering if I will be sitting out the storm alone, I am joined by a small flock of titmice, all twittering in the craggy limbs above my head.

Hearing the rain against my poncho, feeling it splash against my naked face, I imagine it beading up, running down my nose the way it runs along the ridges of the palms. For some reason this thought makes me smile, and I turn my face to catch the rain full force.

What, I wonder, would Miss Anderson say if she saw me now? Suddenly, prompted by this midmorning storm, I catch myself thinking of my first grade teacher, a raw-boned woman given to wearing sturdy lace-up shoes and a sober look. More specifically, I think back to the day in 1957 when rows of eager six-year-olds ran to the cantilevered windows of our classroom to stare at the pouring rain.

Miss Anderson, undone by the disruption, was livid.

"Sit down, children!" she frantically commanded in her thin, high voice. "You've seen rain before." And so we had.

Returning to our desks, we did as we were told—opened our books, put our feet on the cool tile floor, and read. Distractions, we were learning, were not allowed.

But here, beneath this low, gray Texas sky, I follow distractions like threads. The copper-colored grass, the sandy soil, the green jays squawking in the oaks—each distracts me from my life as an adult. I am, for the moment at least, six again, childlike, playing in the rain.

"You've got to be carefully taught," sang Deborah Kerr as Anna in the film *The King and I*. And like many children raised in the fifties and early sixties, I was taught to stay on task, to do my work before I thought of play. It's not a bad lesson, of course, but simply one that doesn't wash. What my heart told me then, and still tells me now, is that work is just another way to play.

And so, for days now, I have walked these trails at Lebh Shomea, walked in wind and sun and rain, walked entirely off task. A retreat center where people from all over the country come to rest and read and pray, this place, I have learned, is also a place to play.

"To play," Hugo Rahner writes in *Man at Play*, "is to yield oneself to a kind of magic, to enact to oneself the absolute other, to pre-empt the future, to give the lie to the inconvenient world of fact." In play, he argues, the mind accepts what is "unimagined and incredible"; it enters a place where none of the usual pressures matter—not time, not space, not the limits of human understanding.

To accept the unimagined and incredible—that, in a sense, is what I'm doing as I walk these sandy trails.

Earlier this morning, for instance, before the rain blew in from somewhere in the Gulf, I spent more time than any grown-up should watching a pair of beetles on this narrow path. Lowly dung beetles, the two had been struggling with a deer pellet, pushing it off to who knows where. Crawling atop the lump, which was roughly twice their size, each beetle would turn around once, hop down to the sand head-first, and then begin kicking with its strong hind legs. Every few seconds or so, the two tumblebugs would find themselves out of sync and have to begin again. It looked like a tedious process, and a hopeless one as well.

And yet, all up and down the trail, other creatures like these two were hard at work. Usually laboring alone, hosts of dung beetles were rolling the droppings of last night's deer somewhere. They were tidying up the earth.

Had I ever noticed them before? I had, but I'd never noted that they do their work in reverse.

What happens to these little balls of dung is something I know only from reading William Bryant Logan's description in *Dirt: The Ecstatic Skin of the Earth*. Noting that there are more than 120 species of dung beetles, Logan explains that after an individual has taken the dung into her burrow, she uses it not only as food for herself but also as a growing medium for her young. It is out of this "dung's heart," as Logan calls it, that the next generation is born.

An unappetizing scenario, perhaps, but one I thought of as I squatted on that sandy path, watching those beetles at work. Nature's economy, one could call it, the riotous recycling of all that falls to the earth.

This may be serious business for the dung beetles, but for me it is a reprieve—from thought, from time, from the weight of my own earnest self.

It is in these moments of simple delight that the world expands, diaphanous, glinting like a spider web at dawn. Only the willing eye is keen enough to perceive such a radical change; only the playful life is large enough to engage it.

The Subtle Signs
of Spring

STICKS AND LICHENS and little bits of fur—even now, with spring still a month or so away, the nest building has begun.

It was just a week ago, while sitting at the computer in my study, that I first saw the pair of Carolina wrens flying in and out of the tiny house that has hung in our front yard for years. Trilling among the trees, flitting from elbowbush to Mexican oregano to Turk's cap, they had skittered from one flimsy perch to the next.

Finally, after working their way from the roots of an upturned stump to the trunk of a larger oak, they had taken turns investigating the hollow gourd that dangles beside the path.

Two summers ago, that same gourd had been home to a pair of black-crested titmice. Will it be filled with baby wrens this year?

Curious, I turn off my computer, grab a sack of sunflower seeds, and head outside. My objective, at least on the surface, is to fill the two empty feeders in front of my study window. In reality, I want to see the nest.

Standing on the gravel path that makes a loop around our house, I duck my head, steady the gourd with my fingertips, and peek inside. On more than one occasion when I've done this, I've been met by the rush of wings. Today, however, there seems to be no one home.

Whether this pile of sticks and lichens is a real nest, or just a practice run, is something I can't know. Neither can I know for sure whether the slender strand of fur running through it is a piece of last year's nest, pulled out when I emptied the house in the fall.

"Look," I had said to my husband, holding the contents lightly in my hand. "It's Happy's." Months after our cocker spaniel had died, her silky fur had reappeared as bedding for a baby bird. And woven tightly through it, I saw, were threads of black and brown—the legacy of our tortoiseshell cat, now gone as well. This year the wrens have found these little tufts of fur, discarded in the flowerbed below. The wrens have given them another life.

Or so I like to think.

After these fifty-plus days of winter, these weeks without rain and these days of bone-chilling cold, I am anxious for the spring. Any day now, I suspect, the narcissus and daffodils will open. And almost any day now, the Mexican buckeyes and the redbuds will all be awash in pink.

Already, in fact, blue hyacinths are blooming in the little copse of oak beside the drive. Already, the scent of winter honeysuckle drifts in waves across the lawn.

The earth is beginning to stir.

Watching the goldfinches feeding on the bag of thistle at my window, or the chickadees flitting nervously from tree to tree, I have trouble sitting still. In these lengthening days of almost-spring, these days when sun is bringing last year's garden back to life, I can feel my own life, too.

Walking through my bare front yard, where the bur oak and the Chinese pistache and the desert willow have stood leafless now for months, I am drawn to what I know is still alive. The rosette of leaves at the base of the frozen salvia, the bloom on the Spanish moss, the sworls of green where I dropped the seeds of larkspur and cosmos and phlox last fall—"The Lord God is subtle," Einstein said, and so is almost-spring.

Unspectacular as it is, this little plot of land is all the evidence I need that life indeed seeks life. Burned by the cold, battered by the wind, life nonetheless returns. Even what is damaged—the frozen tops of the Mexican marigold mint, the brittle stalks of lemon grass, every dead twig, leaf, and stem—even these refuse, at last, to be undone.

"How hard to realize that every camp of men or beast has this glorious starry firmament for a roof!" John Muir wrote while camping in Alaska in 1890. "In such places standing alone on the mountaintop it is easy to realize that whatever special nests we make—leaves and moss like the marmots and birds, or tents or piled stone—we all dwell in a house of one room—the world with the firmament for its roof—and are sailing the celestial spaces without leaving any track."

Standing under that same sky, under that same roof of sun and stars, I peer into the nest of a tiny bird and think: Can anything be more marvelous, more wondrous, more sublime?

Traveling without Goals

IT IS six thirty on a cool spring evening, and I am stretched out contentedly in the hammock, watching the bare limbs of the live oak responding to my weight.

Only minutes before, I stood at the end of the driveway as my neighbor took off on her second spin around the block. I had joined her through the first lap, but having had my fill of heavy breathing for the day, I declined the invitation to keep on.

Lying here now, I do my best to concentrate on one thing at a time. This minute it is the crisp blue of sky, beginning to thin ever so slightly at the edges. The next it is the scent of mountain laurel, the essence of purple gathering itself like oil on water. Or the clatter of oak leaves scuttling across the metal roof.

For the first time all day, I am content simply to be.

As one writer has put it, though, "We all have a monkey mind," and within seconds, mine is doing cartwheels through the trees. *"I should be fixing dinner,"* I tell myself. "I should be reading. I should be cleaning house." One should leads to another, and before I know it, my monkey mind is hanging by its heels, mocking me with the lines of a poem I haven't heard in years. Given where I am, I have to admit that the title—"Lying in a Hammock at William Duffy's Farm in Pine Island, Minnesota"—seems particularly apropos. Tauntingly, the monkey begins to recite the words of poet James Wright:

Over my head, I see the bronze butterfly,
Asleep on the black trunk,
Blowing like a leaf in green shadow.
Down the ravine behind the empty house,
The cowbells follow one another
Into the distance of the afternoon.
To my right,
In a field of sunlight between two pines,
The droppings of last year's horses
Blaze up into golden stones.
I lean back, as the evening darkens and comes on,
A chicken hawk floats over, looking for home.
I have wasted my life.

My God, I think, that's me. My monkey mind is dangling by its tail, screeching through clenched teeth. It will not be ignored.

Somewhere in the pasture at the bottom of the hill, the rancher who lives nearby is pulling his truck to a stop and sounding his horn. *"Beep, beep, b-e-e-p."* Recognizing this as their dinner call, his cows begin lumbering toward the pickup, bellowing mournfully all the way.

I look up, half expecting to see a chicken hawk drift by, but instead I am greeted by the sight of two black vultures, circling high above the house.

"You are wasting your life," the monkey warns, leering at me from its perch above the hammock. I cover my ears, but it chatters on undeterred.

Naysayer, detractor, cynic—this monkey mind of mine is constantly leading me astray, distracting me, filling my quiet time with its high-pitched prattle. Posing as the voice of reason, it dares me to raise a defense, to justify my idleness, my contentment with the way things are.

"It's un-American," the monkey cries, pelting me with oak galls.

"Where are your goals, your ambitions? Where is your drive?"

"Enough!" I shout, stirring the great limb where the creature balances on one foot.

The monkey merely laughs.

Continually lying in wait, my monkey mind invariably attacks at times like this. In the stillness of a spring evening, in the luxuriant silence of midnight, in the midst of simple pleasures—it is then that the monkey shrieks for more.

What can I say in reply? Closing my eyes, I recall John Tallmadge's "In the Mazes of Quetico," a comparison between mountain climbing and his experiences navigating the waters of Ontario's Quetico Provincial Park.

"Successful canoeing requires you to give up the aims and skills of a mountaineer," Tallmadge writes. "In the first place, you must learn to travel without a goal, for Quetico has no center and promises no summit views."

Whereas mountaineering relies on "fixed landmarks" and "tangible goals," Tallmadge notes that "a canoe trip does not advance so much as it grows, unfolding gradually, like a bud, or pushing on like a root that follows a crack in rock."

Chattering more loudly than ever, my monkey mind cautions against disorientation, against passivity, against what it sees as a dangerous lack of drive.

This time, however, I am not listening. With my eyes fixed on the treetops and my ears tuned to the call of a cardinal overhead, I lean back and let the hammock do its work.

Learning to Love
the World

OFFEE CUP in one hand, notebook in the other, I am sitting
in the archway of an open-air stone chapel, astonished by the
morning.

For twenty minutes now, I have been watching a host of barn swallows sweeping across the dry brown field in front of me, ascending and descending not on wings but on will. Seeming hardly to move their lithe bodies, they rise and fall on waves of imagination, on sunlight, on energy from the earth itself. Their flight, arcing and dipping like the sound of conversation from another room, they glide past me, unbidden and unearned.

They are the simple graces of the morning, these birds that come as unfailingly as dawn.

Taking a sip of coffee, I set down the cup and reach for my binoculars. Across the narrow asphalt road, I have noticed, a large Ashe juniper has come alive with birds—titmouse, cardinal, house finch, mockingbird, scissor-tailed flycatcher, Bewick's wren, starling, and, weaving through them all, the fight-flight of a pair of eastern kingbirds.

They are the extravagances of the morning, these birds that spend themselves like fire, that, like everything beautiful, blaze up, then disappear.

At the base of the tree, in a patch of bare, black earth, a single titmouse has emerged to wrestle with a golden leaf. Barely larger than its prey, the bird picks up an edge and shakes it, picks it up and shakes it. Unsuccessful in wresting the object from the ground, the titmouse finally flits away to the tree again, twittering as it flies.

The leaf still flutters in the dirt. Is it the wind that moves it? Some force that I can't see? What looks like a leaf, I realize at last, is in fact a giant moth.

So, I ask myself, do I move it? Save it? Take it someplace where it won't be threatened by the birds? Resisting the urge to rescue another creature's breakfast, I watch from a distance as the moth twitches for a moment more, then lies completely still. Finally, however, I have to come in closer, have to look, have to bend and stroke the mauve-brown pattern on its velvet wings. It quivers at my touch.

What I am looking at, I discover, is an imperial moth. "Easily recognized by its large size and yellow wings," my guidebook tells me, "variably spotted and shaded with pinkish, orangish, or purplish brown."

Even as I make note of its symmetry and size, I know that there is no forgetting such a sight. Wings spanning a good thirteen centimeters, wings the essence of yellow—could anything be so bright, so delicate, so bold?

They are the audacity of the morning, these wings that dare to call attention to themselves.

Crouching beside the tree, hands resting on my thighs, I watch as the moth moves away from me and skitters toward a patch of brittle grass. In a second, it will be out of my field of vision, and I will turn my attention to the sound of a canyon wren trilling in the trees behind me.

Attention—what more do I have to give the world than that? What more can I do than say *This matters*, listen, look, engage? What more is there to do?

Walking along the asphalt road, walking toward a waterfall of wren song spilling from the trees, I sense that I have made a choice: I have given my assent, my attention, to what is wild, what is beautiful, what is out of my control.

I have said *This matters.*

A year ago, when this place was empty of people, I sat on a bench in the open-air chapel, reading poetry to the caretaker's dog. Stretched out across the flagstone floor, her head between her paws, the ancient Lab appeared to listen as I went from one poem to the next.

I should have felt silly, I suppose, reading Mary Oliver that way. But I didn't.

"There is only one question," I read when I came to the lines entitled "Spring": "how to love this world." One question—I think of that phrase now as I stand in the brilliance of another August morning, cloudless sky above me, dusty ground below.

How do we love the world? Like this, just like this, sitting in the archway of an open-air chapel, touching the wing of a moth, tracing the flight of birds—burrowing below the skin of things, emerging with dust between my toes.

Listening to Owls

JUST AFTER DUSK, a sliver of moon hangs low above the sabal palms. Already, a chorus of pauraques is exchanging calls in the woods beyond the fields of brittle grass. Already, three tiny screech owls wail invisibly from the tree tops, their song as thin and tremulous as the rim of a crystal glass.

Click-click-click-click-click ski-ow! From somewhere in the shadows to my right, a feathered silhouette emerges, dips, then glides below the roof line of the quiet house. Seconds later, the sound returns, doubling back upon itself like waves exploding on an empty beach.

Creature of waste place and pasture, woodland and plain, the barn owl is on the hunt.

"Twice last night I heard a really odd sound, some kind of animal I couldn't place," I had written in a note to Father Kelly Nemeck, the resident priest at Lebh Shomea, two days before. "It sounded like a screaming cat fight, but it was clearly just one animal. Any idea what it was?"

"It could've been a cat," Father Kelly had whispered when he saw me outside the dining room the following night. "There are at least six here." Six varieties, that is.

I had grinned at the very thought.

In the four years that I've been coming to this South Texas retreat center for my spring semester break, I've seen a good bit of wildlife, but never anything that wild. Rio Grande turkeys, javelina, white-tailed deer, Mexican free-tailed bats, raccoons, armadillos, rabbits, and an amazing array of birds—by mid-March, every inch of these eleven hundred acres of oak motte and palm grove and scrub are teeming with a rich melange of life. The prospect of adding this mystery creature to my list was simply too good to let pass.

And so, waiting until dark, I had grabbed my flashlight, quietly closed my door, and padded down the stairs toward the porch below. By this time of night, most of the other guests in the Big House were resting in their rooms or browsing through the first floor library. I sensed I was all alone.

Click-click-click-click-click ski-ow! Somewhere in the distance, the creature was already on the move. Coming from behind the house at first, the sound seemed to travel around the far end of the veranda, out to the deer pasture near the road, then off into the woods beyond the lawn. This was no cat, I finally admitted to myself. No, it had to be a bird, but this scream was nothing that I'd ever heard before.

Sitting on a bench at the corner of the house, I had listened as the creature came and went, came and went. Still, though, I had not seen a thing.

Before long, the sound disappeared as well. Except for the wind rattling in the tops of the palms, and the pauraques calling in the distance, the night was suddenly silent. The world was silent. I stood, flicked on my light, and took a step back toward the porch.

Ski-ow! From the live oak right beside me, a bird erupted with a scream, stretched its long, scalloped wings, and floated toward the woods. I knew I'd seen an owl.

Through the rain of the next two days, I searched the books for clues. Long wings. Catlike scream. Clicking sound in flight. It wasn't much to go on, but this list of traits I'd noted in my journal was at least a place to start. Eliminating the handful of owls I'd seen or heard before—great horned owl, screech owl, barred owl, burrowing owl—and checking the names of species known to live nearby, I narrowed the field to two.

As I discovered, it was either a short-eared owl or a barn owl I'd been hearing these last few days. Only when I checked *The Book of Owls* by Lewis Wayne Walker did I know for sure which one.

"The screech uttered by Barn Owls is explosive, and aside from its short duration it might be compared to a pre-diesel locomotive letting off steam," Walker writes. "When a Barn Owl is flying high in the air, completely undisturbed, it will often utter this call every half minute or so and with such volume that it may be heard for a half mile or more. . . . Another note is seemingly used when a pair of Barn Owls are flying in close proximity, consisting of a series of metallic-sounding clicks."

Knowing what it is I have seen, I leave my room on a moonlit night, walk softly down the stairs, and take a seat outside by the asphalt drive. A trio of screech owls, nesting in woodpecker holes in the tops of the palms, call to one another in front of me. As they have on so many nights before, coyotes sing in the scrubby pasture miles away toward the beach. Pauraques and poorwills weave a net of voices in response.

Carried on the wind, sounds come from places they are not. Lost in shadows, shapes blur, grow indistinct, merge. It is easy, in such a space, on such a night, to imagine things, to let the mind convince itself it knows more than it does. It is easy to think that mystery is held at bay by a flashlight beam, that what is known about is truly known.

Sitting on a wooden bench, under the sliver of a mid-March moon, I hear the words of Wendell Berry playing in my head. "To go in the dark with a light is to know the light," he writes. "To know the dark, go dark. Go without sight, / and find that the dark, too, blooms and sings, / and is traveled by dark feet and dark wings."

A mile from here, a raccoon is leaving her footprints in the moist earth beside a fence. A deer is tensing at the howl of a coyote. A flock of turkeys is settling in for the night in a motte of oaks.

From around the corner of the house comes a now familiar *click-click-click-click-click*. And then a scream. And then the silence of wings passing once, twice over my unprotected head.

Energy from the Earth

I AM SITTING in the car outside a convenience store, waiting for my husband to return with a jar of crunchy peanut butter, when suddenly it dawns on me: One day, perhaps even in my lifetime, this parking lot will cease to be.

Squinting into the sun, I imagine what will happen when the stand of bamboo next door sends its roots farther and farther under the asphalt, what will happen when the surface begins to crack and buckle and wear away.

I smile at the very thought.

It is perverse, no doubt, but frequently I entertain myself with visions of grass consuming intersections, frontage roads, strip centers, malls. I console myself with thoughts of live oaks bursting through foundations, stretching out of windows, crashing up through roofs. I dream of unencumbered earth.

How much of the land mass of the continental United States is buried under concrete, asphalt, and other forms of impervious cover? "Good question," a geographer I know tells me when I call to ask. He doesn't have a clue.

The answer is elusive, all right, but knowing that there are four million miles of roads and highway in this country, and knowing that every new superstore, every new driveway, every new warehouse and fast food restaurant entombs another patch of earth, I also know that we are losing touch with the force that animates life.

Sealed for our protection, a little more soil each year is doomed to die.

Like most kids, writer William Bryant Logan spent a good part of his early childhood digging holes in vacant lots. In fact, together with his young friend Stephanie, he writes in *Dirt: The Ecstatic Skin of the Earth*, he once labored for quite some time in hopes of reaching China.

I can't say that I ever had such a goal myself, but I do recall how thrilling it was to find a fresh load of dirt dumped somewhere in the neighborhood. Ripe for climbing up or sliding down, such a pile invariably attracted every ten-year-old for blocks.

Even more appealing, though, was the trench that appeared one day in my friend Lee's backyard. Dug to replace an aging sewer line, it was fair game once the workmen left each afternoon at five.

"We can be the Mole People," Lee announced as we crouched there in the cool, damp earth. Having covered sections of the chest-deep trench with plywood, we were comfortably hidden from the outside world—and any of the kids we didn't want to see.

Living as we did on the edge of town, we were also blessed with a creek that ran behind my house; with an abandoned sewage plant which, while strictly off-limits, attracted us with its spans of rusty pipe; with a wood that bordered our little neighborhood on both the east side and the south.

It was into this wood that all of us—not just Lee and I, but also Sherrie and Vicki, Debbie and Carol, Robert and Darrell—would hike each summer when the dewberry vines were full. And it was there, at more temperate times of the year, that we would dare each other to go to the "haunted house."

"Wait for me!" I would always end up yelling when my braver friends took off without me. Running from the cover of trees toward the sagging wooden porch, I was terrified of tripping in one of the holes we were sure had been dug in the yard for us, of entangling myself in one of the ancient rose bushes guarding the corners of the faded house.

The terror was delicious, and it ended all too soon.

By the mid-1960s, what was left of the house had been razed, the roses and many of the trees had been bulldozed, and the land had been platted for the city's newest homes. Another patch of ground was being paved.

"You know, there's energy in the earth," I heard a woman say not long ago. "Haven't you felt it after standing in a certain place?"

Of course, I thought as I listened to her speak, of course I have.

Recently, while taking a walk on a moonlit Texas night, I found myself sitting cross-legged on the ground, the palms of my hands pressed hard against the supple grass. Electrified by stars, electrified by the earth beneath my feet, I knew that they and I were products of a single source, that they and I were kin.

What happens when we never touch the earth, when all we know of soil is what we see along the edges of our parking lots, when nature is just a force to be subdued?

When Moses beholds the burning bush, William Bryant Logan recalls in *Dirt*, "God tells Moses, 'Take off your shoes, because the ground where you are standing is holy ground.' He is asking Moses to experience in his own body what the burning bush experiences: a living connection between heaven and earth, the life that stretches out like taffy between our father sun and our mother the earth.

"If you do not believe this," Logan advises, "take off your shoes and stand in the grass or in the sand or in the dirt."

The charge is almost more than we can bear.

The Season of Empty Nests and Hope

RAIN. After months of drought, months of dust building up on the car, on the roof, on the windows of our little house, even this thirty-minute drenching brings relief. Rain. Even the word refreshes.

Standing silent on the porch, my husband and I watch as water runs down the drive and pools up level with the step. Like us, the wide-eyed cat in the doorway seems to have forgotten what rain looks like, sounds like, smells like. Like us, he has learned to live with drought.

For the better part of the morning, until the thunder rolls off toward the south, we keep the windows open, listening, wanting more. By noon, we sense the storm is over. Cool recedes. Heat rises from the grass. There is no air.

As if by instinct, as if some memory of rain still lingers in a corner of my brain, I head outside to see exactly what the storm has done. Already, the world looks greener. The ox-eye daisies, wilted the night before, stand firm and tall. The lyre-leaf sage, once shriveled down to half its normal size, lifts red-veined leaves up toward the sun. The *Gerbera* daisy, a small inheritance from my mother's yard, swells, unfurls itself above the rain-soaked earth.

The world is changing right before my eyes.

Taking the gravel path that begins to the left of the driveway and makes a loop around the house, I move from bed to bed, just looking, taking stock of how things are. I note, for example, that the Mexican oregano is in full bloom, that the pavonia is flowering, that the prairie beard tongue has gone to seed. I note, as well, the patch of horsemint growing—quite unexpectedly—among the spent gaillardias, the one Texas thistle blooming near the drive, the prostrate winecup, hanging on.

It is during this routine inventory that I spot the little birdhouse lying on the ground. Blown from its limb by the storm, the gourd is almost hidden in the tangle of groundcover and shrubs, almost missed among the vinca and the sage.

Two months ago, at least, I had watched from my study window as this year's pair of Bewick's wrens prepared their nest inside this hollow gourd. Periodically, standing in the yard or on the drive, I had heard what sounded like the chirping cry of baby birds. And then all action stopped.

Had I scared the wrens away? Or had they simply raised their brood and left? Afraid to peer too closely inside, afraid that some-thing might still be living there, I had given the gourd a wide berth every time I passed. Just in case, I thought optimistically. But now, here it lies, waterlogged and already filled with pillbugs. Clearly, the nest is ruined.

Curious to learn what a wren might see as good material to fill its house, I pick up the gourd and carry it to a nearby bench. There, ten-tatively and with care, I begin to pull out the contents piece by piece.

First come the twigs, most of which are too long to fit through the hole straight on; only by turning them at an angle, I realize, could a bird have brought them in. Next come the little bits of lichen and the gray-green shreds of moss. Is that a strand of the Spanish moss I hung near the birdhouse earlier this spring? It certainly looks to be.

Now, with the nest's framework out of the way, I can inch my fin-gers a little deeper into the house, pulling out a tangled mass of fibers and feathers and fluff. Spreading it out on the bench, I begin picking it apart, separating each component from the next.

Oak leaves, some shredded, some whole; a single white hair; the textured end off a cellophane candy wrapper; gummy wads of spider web; several white cocoons; the blue pull-string off a pack of mints; a strip of someone's plastic produce bag, printed with the words "Tear Here"; a spider's egg sac; bits of matted fur; and feathers—downy gray feathers with tan on the ends, tiny blue jay feathers, white feathers, brown feathers, and one dappled like stone, perhaps from the mother wren herself.

At last, when the house is almost empty, I can peer inside to see the lone abandoned egg. White with brown flecks, it is barely the size of my little finger nail. Rolling out, it hits the ground even before I see it fall.

"'Hope' is the thing with feathers," said Emily Dickinson. Indeed, it is hope I feel as I set the broken egg on the bench beside the pile of tiny feathers, as I hang the empty birdhouse head-high from a nearby tree, as I imagine the scent of rain.

In Ordinary Time

ENDING SLOWLY, as if taking my eyes off the creature will cause it to disappear, I lay down my trowel and gloves, turn toward the house, and walk as softly as I can, being careful not to stir up the gravel path beneath me as I move. Because the wooden door is swollen with moisture from the recent rains, it squeaks when I turn the handle and push. I grimace at the sound.

"Get the glasses," I tell my husband quietly. Accustomed to my cryptic instructions, he puts down his magazine, grabs the two sets of binoculars we keep on the chest by the back door, and follows me outside.

Within seconds, we are standing beneath the giant hackberry that grows at the edge of the woods.

"Green heron?" I speculate, noting the chestnut-colored head, shaggy black crest, and bright orange legs.

"Um," my husband replies, focusing his glasses on the crow-sized bird. Out of the corner of my eye, I can see him smile.

Perched with its back to us all this time, the bird finally turns a fraction to one side, giving us our first look at its weaponlike beak and glowing golden eyes. If we've had any doubts up to now, this resolves them in a flash. We're watching a green heron, all right.

What makes this sighting so odd is that the bird is out of place. Common as it is in Central Texas, the green heron is typically found near water—a pond, a river, a stream—not in suburban back yards.

Speculating as to what has brought it to our woods, we imagine that the creature is on its way to a stock tank somewhere down the road or, given the fact it sometimes nests away from water, that it's looking for a place to raise its young. Indeed, the color of its legs, which turn from yellow to orange during the breeding season, is a difficult clue to miss.

In general, though, the green heron draws little attention to itself. A dark bird, and more squatty than its kin, it could easily have passed as but a shadow in our hackberry tree. Had it not been for the *skyow!* the bird let out several times while I was working nearby, I would probably have missed it altogether. But agitated as it was—by the cats, perhaps, or the flock of resident jays—it let its presence be known.

And now, as we stand watching, it turns its back on us again and issues a final *skyow!* before taking off through the trees. We lose sight of it at once.

What is it that we've seen? Exchanging puzzled yet satisfied looks, my husband and I walk to the house in silence. We know the creature's name, know its habitat and habits, but we don't know how it fits. What does it mean to have such a bird in your woods, to have it sitting there, jaylike, in the commonest of trees?

Years ago, when we lived in a small house in town, my husband and I were frequently surprised by what showed up in our tiny back yard. Once while looking for warblers in the trees, I found myself watching a pileated woodpecker instead. Nearly twenty inches tall, this black and white bird with the bright red crest had announced itself with a series of *kuk-kuk-kukkuks* as it inched up the trunk of a pecan. Never before had I seen one of these amazing birds, and I've never seen one since.

Equally odd was the creature that lived for a time in the storeroom off our carport. I can't remember who saw it first, or exactly what we saw, but I suspect it was the eyes. Or perhaps the tail. The creature we called Ringo stayed at our house for weeks, hiding by day in a narrow space between the shelves above our washer and coming out only when it thought we weren't around.

Somewhere we had heard that ringtails like dry dog food and bananas, and so every night we left an offering of sorts. Every morning it was gone. Occasionally, when we flipped on the light to leave the food, we would see Ringo staring out between the shelves. Less often still, we would catch the animal perched on the frame above the door or leaping across the room to its lair.

Invariably, though, we would hear it every night. Not sure at first what we were hearing, we finally realized that the rolling sound was the sound of dog food pellets being batted across the storeroom shelf, as if the creature were playing a game.

What is it that we've seen? Two weeks into what the church calls ordinary time, that time when nothing special happens, I sit at my window and watch. Day after day, the same gluttonous squirrel comes to raid the feeder, and day after day he loses his balance and falls. The same cardinals, the same wrens, the same pair of Inca doves walking chickenlike down the limb—they are all here too. It is an ordinary time indeed.

And yet, if I turn my head just right, tune my ears just so, suspend belief about what should and should not be, amazing birds appear in the commonest of trees. Unfamiliar songs break the silence of a summer day. And everywhere, the world looks back at me with dark, astonished eyes.

Harvesting Seeds
of Trust

TODAY I AM harvesting wildflower seeds. Snapping the dried heads off this spring's poppies, breaking the stems of the Drummond's phlox between my thumb and forefinger, I make a little heap of pods in my open palm. Then, crushing them one by one, I fling their almost invisible seed across the sunny lawn.

Fine as dust, some of it lands on the still blooming gaillardia. Another handful falls in the wake of a bee as it rises from an open winecup.

Were I a more careful gardener, or at least a tidier one, I would pay closer attention to where the seed drops. I would plan and calculate, considering the drift of the wind, the gentle slope of the soil, the direction of water washing across the lawn.

But I am not so careful as that.

Instead, I stand at the edge of the drive and throw, watching as some of the seed blows into the path, some into the street. These are the seeds of next year's accidents, well-intentioned beauties out of place.

In another two weeks, maybe three, the last of the gaillardia and bachelor's button will be gone. The Texas thistle, greenthread, larkspur, horsemint—all the spring color will be gone. Already, in fact, last winter's grass has mellowed to a golden brown. Heavy with seed, it droops amid the flowers and gives the lawn an unkempt look.

I no long worry what the neighbors will think.

Today, in the comfort of an air-conditioned room, a friend and I are having a conversation about trust, about how we trust not just each other but all that is.

"What does it mean?" I ask her, not intending to be dense. "Where do we begin?"

Sitting quietly for a moment, she appears to roll the question around in her mind before answering.

"Go out to your garden," she tells me at last. It is all she has to say.

For what? I find myself wondering later in the day. To see where newly hatched grasshoppers have left the hibiscus leaves in shreds? To trace the route of the armadillo that rumbles through the garlic rows each night? To feel the sting of mosquitoes trying their luck on my ankles and down the backs of my sun-starved legs? Is this what my friend, my fellow gardener, wishes me to learn?

"I alternate between thinking of the planet as home—dear and familiar stone hearth and garden—and as a hard land of exile in which we are all sojourners," Annie Dillard writes in her essay "Sojourner." "Today I favor the latter view."

Some days, I too am struck by the foreignness of things, by the randomness and chaos of it all. "It doesn't seem to be here that we belong," Dillard admits, "here where space is curved, the earth is round, we're all going to die, and it seems as wise to stay in bed as budge."

One day my flowers are tall, erect, turning their brilliant faces to the sun; the next they are waterlogged and limp, pressed to the ground by a storm. Touched by life's vagaries, by the sheer capriciousness of sun and season, I wade through the garden, undoing what weather has done. Cautiously, I untangle stem from stem, bloom from bloom, urging each mangled plant to set itself aright.

It is the eternal quest for order, impatience gone awry.

"I think half the time we do live in chaos," my gardening friend tells me in a letter, "yet at the heart of it is T. S. Eliot's 'still point of the turning world.' It's one of those both/ands again."

Standing at the edge of the garden, flinging seeds into the wind, I am struck by my sudden willingness to risk, to let what is going to happen happen. In this one act, at least, I am pleased to cultivate disorder, to invite surprise.

How do we learn to trust apparent chaos, to live in the wake of small diminishments as well as plenty? How do we learn to love what we can't control as much as what we can?

Go out to your garden, my friend tells me. That is the place to begin.

On Holy Ground

IT IS JUST after midnight when the nine of us—seven college students, another sponsor and I—stretch out on a large concrete terrace to watch for shooting stars. Lying head to toe a hundred feet or so above the Frio River, our eyes on the eastern sky, we are bathed in moonlight, bathed in the silver silence of an August night.

"That's Venus," someone finally says, as if answering a question no one has asked. Straight ahead of us, sixty degrees or so above the tree line, hangs a glowing planet. "Third brightest object in the sky," my *Field Guide to the Night Sky* says of Venus. Known as Phosphorus (from the Greek for "light bringer") and Hesperus (from the Latin for "vesper"), it is both the evening and the morning star, seen just after sunset and just before the dawn.

But it is midnight, I remind myself. And what we are looking at, I will later learn, is actually the planet Jupiter, not quite so bright as Venus, though many times as large.

Misidentified or not, though, this planet will be for us a kind of guide.

"Watch the area just below it," another voice tells us. "That's where you'll see the shooting stars."

Lying above the canyon, my head pressed against the hard slab, my feet nudging the shoulders of a student I can't see, I train my eyes on a cloudless summer sky. Twenty miles from the nearest town of any size, we are awash tonight in stars. Not even the light of the gibbous moon, poised above the south end of the canyon, can spoil such a heavenly view.

"I can't believe I'm twenty-one and I've never seen a shooting star," one of the students suddenly confesses, breaking the silence yet again. "Me neither," I add reluctantly, though I've had more than twice as many years to look for one.

How had I missed seeing them? Was I not attentive enough?

It is August 14, two days after the supposed climax of the Perseid meteor shower. While scientists may be concentrating on discovering unknown planets or sending a space probe to Mars, this is one of the most spectacular shows in the galaxy—and it requires nothing but patience and time.

The cause of this phenomenon, I have read, is the passage of the comet Swift-Tuttle, which enters our solar system every 130 years or so. What we're seeing in this most famous of all meteor showers is actually the comet's path, its trail of dust and debris.

If I am lucky, there could be as many as eighty meteors an hour tonight, eighty chunks of cosmic rock blazing across the sky at twenty miles a second before burning up for good. If I am not lucky, there could be as few as four.

"I saw one!" a student exclaims from somewhere on the deck. Immediately, I become more vigilant. Scanning the sky, I imagine invisible lights, undiscovered planets, galaxies far beyond our own. Straining, I attempt to see what no eye can.

As much as anything, it is the sound of a collective gasp, the sound of my own astonishment, that jolts me from my reverie. From some-where in the constellation Perseus comes a ray of brilliant light. Moving left to right across a field of stars, it burns itself into the sky, into the skin of my imagination. I flinch out of sheer surprise.

I have seen a shooting star at last.

Hours from now, when the sun begins to set again behind the cedar-studded hills, the students and I will walk down to the river for an evening swim. There, wearing tennis shoes or sandals to protect our feet, we will walk out on the naked rocks, will wade, jump, fling ourselves into the current, will let the water take us where it will.

Embraced by walls of limestone, we will float on the remnants of a prehistoric sea.

Deposited first as part of the Glen Rose formation, and then as Edwards limestone, the rock here is the vestige of a warm Cretaceous body of water, the same shallow sea that covered all of Texas millions of years ago. Uplifted several thousand feet during the Miocene age, this region has since been worn away by streams, leaving a riverbed of underlying Glen Rose rock.

It is this rock that will feel so slick beneath our wary feet, this rock that, in the magical refraction of clear water, will seem much closer—or farther—than it really is.

While the students let themselves be washed downstream, pausing to paint themselves with a greenish clay one of them has dug out of the bank, I will find a hollow in this rock. There, while the water cascades around my shoulders, I will hear myself breathing for the first time in months. I will remember my place on the earth.

For the ancient Pueblo peoples, whose kivas dot the American Southwest, the sipapu was the portal through which spirits entered the human world above. I will think of this fact as I sit here in the Frio River, in this flowing fissure in the earth. I will think, too, of my own connections to this place, of the imprint its smells and textures left on my senses as a child, of the family stories carried in these stones.

This is where life starts, the water and rocks will tell me. This is where you start.

Is there such a thing as holy ground? Sitting in this river—star dust blazing trails above me, star dust washed away beneath my feet—I know that there is nothing else.

Icons of Loss and Grace

I

Five weeks after my mother's death, I am standing on the rim of Colorado's Black Canyon, looking down on some of the oldest rock formations in the world—basement rocks, the geologists call them. Clutching the guardrail, I am tempted to lean over the edge and gaze at the Gunnison River below, but at the last minute, something holds me back. Perhaps it is the knowledge that all that separates me from the canyon floor is a waist-high wire fence—and two thousand feet of air.

Why am I doing this? I wonder, taking a seat on a nearby rock. What is it that I've come to find?

The answer, I suspect, lies not so much in logic as in an inexplicable psychic need, in a craving for extremes, for height and depth and the sense of finitude they bring. A long-time acrophobe, I am never more uncomfortable than when standing at the brink of some great chasm or when navigating switchbacks on a shelflike mountain road.

But that's part of the answer as well.

Canyons, like all marginal landscapes, have much to teach. And I, unpracticed student that I am, have come to this place to learn.

Situated between the West Elk Mountains to the north, the Sawatch Range to the east, and the San Juan Mountains to the south, the Black Canyon stretches fifty-three miles through dry and scrubby terrain. Known as the Gunnison Uplift, this rough plateau was formed millions of years ago when a fault line shifted and caused a block of ancient rock to breach the surface of the earth.

Some ten to fifteen million years later, volcanic eruptions would change the course of the still-young Gunnison River, forcing it into its present route across this broad and rugged plain. There it would easily cut through layers of volcanic and sedimentary rock, through shale and sandstone laid down by a long-gone inland sea.

To wear away the ancient schist and gneiss below would take two million years. Even at its peak spring flow of twelve thousand cubic feet a second, the Gunnison could erode this metamorphic rock just an inch a century—or, as the National Park Service puts it, "the width of a human hair each year."

Slow though it would be, the river would ultimately carve a canyon more than two thousand feet in depth. Narrow due to the lack of strong tributaries scouring its sides, the Black Canyon of the Gunnison would become a vertical rift in the earth, its sheer rock walls among the highest in the state.

Even now, more than a century after the first recorded human excursion to the canyon floor, it is hardly an inviting place. Picturesque? Yes. Stunning? Of course. But nonetheless a landscape hard enough to test the nerve of any climber bent on entering its depths.

It is just the sort of space I need.

II

I had never meant to keep a journal of my mother's death, and yet the act came naturally. Night after night I'd come home from the hospital, sit in the old platform rocker in her living room, and record the events of the day. What did the doctors say? Who visited or called? How did my mother feel?

The cancer had been diagnosed in the middle of June, two weeks after my daughter's high school graduation, two weeks after the worry and fear began. The first clue had been my mother's lack of appetite on graduation day. Soon afterward came the pain in her neck and back. Having planned to stay with us for at least a week, she had left after just four days.

Back in the city where she'd lived for many years, her doctor would order tests, and the tests would come back fine—at first. But there would be more pain, and more tests, and eventually someone would say the word: tumor.

June 12: A doctor my mother has never seen before comes in to give her the news. He is the doctor on call, a stranger, a man she believes has no right to tell her things like this. Her hospital gown flapping behind her, my mother chases this stranger from her room. "I don't want to see that man again!" she yells in the direction of the nurse. "How dare he be the one to tell me this."

Two weeks later, we would take my mother home.

Unable to eat, she would grow more frail by the day.

June 26: Shortly after going to sleep, I'm awakened by a noise coming from my mother's room. She has gotten out of bed alone. "Call me," I tell her, fearing she will fall. And so she does—call me, that is. First at 5:00 and then at 6:00 A.M., I hear my mother's voice. "What time is it?" she wants to know. The pain is getting worse.

For the next three days, my sister and I take turns attending to our mother's needs. Who will care for her in the months to come, we wonder? We talk about arrangements, about where she will live, what she will do. And then the conversation stops.

My mother is readmitted to the hospital four days after going home. On Saturday, three and a half quarts of fluid are drained from her abdomen. On Sunday, she calls requesting that I bring her toothbrush when I visit later in the day.

When the tears finally come, I am standing in the video department of the local grocery store, holding a movie that I'll watch and then forget.

It is Monday morning when the chemotherapy begins. "Palliative treatment," the doctor calls it. "Grasping at straws," I want to say. I keep my thoughts to myself.

Later in the day, when the morphine finally dulls her pain, my mother sleeps. "Be sure to pay the bills on time," she'd said before she nodded off. "And put the stamps back in the drawer, else I'll never find them."

June 29: Death rises from the feet. I learn this from my mother's doctor, a man who has watched it come like this before. "The blood is moving to the center of her body," he tells us. "It's like circling the wagons for the end."

My mother's breathing has been labored most of the day, but by evening, it begins to slow down, grow more quiet. When it stops, we hardly notice at all. Death has come as easily as that, like the last bit of air escaping from a child's balloon.

In the end, there is no sound, save the scraping of a chair across linoleum, the swinging open of a door, the quiet summons for a nurse.

III

The mountains wouldn't do this year—at least not the sort of mountains we had been to in the past. There could be no gentle slopes, no grassy meadows, no lakes at the end of a trail. I needed something more austere than that.

I needed an abyss, a chasm for my pain.

The idea that entering desolate places can be a numinous, even cleansing experience is borne out in a host of sacred texts. Moses flees into the desert and finds God in a burning bush. Jesus seeks solitude in the Galilean wilderness, and emerges as a stronger man. The desert fathers and mothers reject their old way of life to live simply in a barren landscape, somehow gaining wisdom in the trade.

But it isn't wisdom that I hope to find at the Black Canyon of the

Gunnison, no answer to the question "why?" What I'm looking for, I suspect, is something with which to identify, something I can see/hear/touch and say: "That's it. That's what I am right now."

A poet might call this phenomenon the objective correlative, that physical reality that suggests a state of mind, that evokes some deep emotion in the one who watches or reads. But that isn't it at all.

I need nothing to evoke the pain and emptiness I feel, nothing to elicit numbness, shock, rage. What I need is a mirror, something I can look into and see myself reflected back.

Describing her attraction to the pueblo communities of the desert Southwest, artist Meinrad Craighead writes, "When I came to New Mexico in 1960, I found the land which matched my interior landscape. The door separating inside and outside opened. What my eyes saw meshed with images I carried in my body."

In short, she recognized herself.

Like attracted to like, emptiness seeking its own—gazing into the Black Canyon is for me not only an exercise in that sort of recognition; it is also an act of expression, a way of giving form to that which has no form, a way of depicting the void.

For centuries, men and women of faith have approached the Unknown not by assaulting it with questions but by sitting in silence at its feet. Language, they knew, had its limits; reason, they knew, its constraints. To progress toward the Ineffable required not inordinate strength of will but a simple willingness to wait, to listen, and, feeling totally unprepared, to enter the desert unarmed.

Living with Mystery, they realized, was exactly that—living with, living in. Such an experience was the antithesis of an intellectualized faith. It was concrete, visceral, and altogether out of their control.

It was awesome in the truest sense of the word.

Ironically, Belden Lane notes in *The Solace of Fierce Landscapes*, while these apophatic mystics rejected all images of God as inadequate, they "[made] an exception in using the imagery of threatening places

as a way of challenging the ego and leaving one at a loss for words."
As Lane puts it, "It is impossible for human intelligence to comprehend God, yet certain places may allow people to experience the necessary risk that opens them, body and soul, to what their minds
cannot entertain."

Like the icon that is both itself and more than itself, such landscapes draw us deep into a mystery we can't penetrate alone. They are
the door between our inside and outside lives. They are liminal places,
spaces fraught with terror, but also filled with grace.

They are places of letting go.

In her prose poem "West Wind," Mary Oliver writes: "When you
hear, a mile away and still out of sight, the churn of the water as it
begins to swirl and roil, fretting around the sharp rocks—when you
hear that unmistakable pounding—when you feel the mist on your
mouth and sense ahead the embattlement, the long falls plunging and
steaming—then row, row for your life toward it."

Drawn to the canyon's edge, I look across the gorge toward Painted
Wall, that mammoth slab of metamorphic rock crisscrossed with
veins of feldspar, mica, and quartz. It is natural to feel quite small in
such a place; it is natural to be afraid.

IV

"There are no trails into the canyon," I overhear the ranger explaining
to a man intent on going in, "only what could at best be referred to as
'routes.'"

Later, catching my breath as I hike along the rim, I can appreciate
her words. And yet, I'll admit, I understand that hiker's urge to
clamber down into the rift, to leave the tourist throngs behind and
wend his way toward something elemental, something primitive and
wild.

Five weeks after my mother's death, my grief still raw, still new, I have come to the Black Canyon to be consoled not by the beauty of the world but by its lack of need for me. In these primeval stones, this depth, this dark and brooding space, I find a place where I am free to be expendable. I find a place where I can practice my own death.

Recalling Andrew Harvey's pilgrimage to northern India, and the impact that this landscape had on him, Belden Lane writes: "Most compelling to his imagination was the fact that the awesome beauty of this fierce land was in no way conditioned by his own frail presence. It was not there for him." Overwhelmed by what he had seen, Lane notes, Harvey could reach only one conclusion: "We are saved in the end by the things that ignore us. . . . In the frightening experience of having our fragile egos ignored, we're thrust beyond fear to a grace unexpected."

Standing on the rim of the Black Canyon, I sense my own contingency in a way I never have before. Like the mule deer and the Gambel oaks, the serviceberry and the marmots sunning themselves on the hot rocks below me, I am a creature formed of elemental earth. That this should comfort me feels strange at first, but such is the nature of grace.

Trusting life, trusting death—at this time and in this place, the two have become as one.

There is peace in the indifference of the world, I have realized. There is peace in knowing it goes on.

V

Eight months have passed now since my mother's death, and though the edge of my grief is less raw, I'm still learning to live with the loss. No—more aptly put, I'm learning to live with Loss, with the thousand empty spaces in the landscape of the soul. A child grows up. A dream goes bad. A body wears out. A parent dies.

It is loss that has brought me once again to Lebh Shomea, to this retreat center where silence is the rule and walking is the way my body learns. Morning, afternoon, and evening, I lose myself on trails cut through the live oak mottes and scrub. Through clearings bright with winecups and groundsel, past huisache trees in bloom, down paths that disappear beneath the sand, I walk.

Sand—why am I surprised to find it here, less than ten miles from the Texas coast? Disturbed by early morning winds, it swirls around me, clinging to my boots, my jeans, my face. With every few steps I take, I stop to brush it off.

Described by the handful of people who live here as a "desert wilderness," this land is, in the purely literal sense at least, neither of those things. Rather, it is part of the extensive Rio Grande Plain that begins just below San Antonio and reaches south to Brownsville. Unlike true desert, which receives no more than ten inches of rain per year, Lebh Shomea and the rest of Kenedy County get roughly twenty-six. That's not a great deal less than the thirty-three inches that annually fall in Central Texas where I live, but it's enough to make the contrast clear.

For the most part, this is brush country. Tangles of mesquite, live oak, yucca, huisache, ebony, mustang grape, and assorted grasses and vines cover much of the county's 1,456.8 square miles. What passes for soil here is in reality millions of years' worth of sand blown inland from the Gulf. In some places, I have read, it is sixty feet in depth.

True desert or not, there is nonetheless a wildness here, a remoteness and desolation that scour the psyche like windblown sand. To prefer such a landscape, I have learned, is to prefer what is hidden, what is fundamental, lean, and spare.

"In desert and mountain wilderness," writes Belden Lane, "people discover liminal places suggesting thresholds between where they have been and where they are going. . . . In whatever form one may find it, 'the desert loves to strip bare,' as Saint Jerome insisted. The desert reduces one to a rawboned simplicity." Clarity, simplicity, the fright-

ening terra firma of the soul—these are what I crave, and these are
what I find in the desert that is Lebh Shomea's heart.

It is just after 8:00 A.M. when I come around a bend in the trail
and stop, surprised by fresh tracks in the sand. Turkey? I ask myself,
studying the curious string of Xs at my feet. A novice when it comes
to reading tracks, I am even more bewildered by the slender furrow
winding S-shaped down the path. Snake? Quite possibly. Tracks,
signs, intimations of something that has come and gone, something
that has been and is no more—these are part of the desert too.

Eight months after my mother's death, my body has begun to
understand the transience of things. It is coming to know that loss,
regardless of its size, is larger than my mind can wrap around. And
cell by cell it is learning that to live with what is absent requires
grounding in the earth; I need to taste it, smell it, hear the echo of its
silence, run my hand across its gritty skin.

Beginning to know myself as part and parcel of the sand beneath
my feet, I am beginning to love the world. I am beginning to love what
is dust.

Acknowledgments

MY DEEPEST THANKS to the friends and colleagues who have made this book possible. I am especially grateful to Scott Slovic for his tireless encouragement and his spirit of generosity; without him, I would have given up on this project long ago. I am thankful, too, for the support of Mary Earle, Marga Speicher, and my husband, Larry, all of whom know intimately the struggles and joys these words represent. Thanks also to the staff of Texas Tech University Press, who saw the potential for this book; to Paul Olson, who helped to give it shape; to my former co-workers at the San Marcos *Daily Record*, where most of these essays first appeared, and my former readers, who gave me the luxury of an audience; to my colleagues at Texas State University–San Marcos who value the literature of place, especially Mark Busby, Dickie Heaberlin, and Priscilla Leder; to the staff of Lebh Shomea for their hospitality and their nurture of wild places; and to those writers whose words have both inspired and challenged me to love and engage the world, particularly Scott Russell Sanders, Mary Oliver, and Wendell Berry.

Finally, I thank Norman Peterson, who would have been thrilled to see this book, and my parents, who first took me to the garden to dig.